ALL BEFORE THEM

ALL BEFORE THEM

Student Opportunities and
Nationally Competitive Fellowships

THE NATIONAL ASSOCIATION OF
FELLOWSHIPS ADVISORS

_____

Edited by Suzanne McCray and Doug Cutchins

THE UNIVERSITY OF ARKANSAS PRESS
FAYETTEVILLE
2015

ISBN 978-1-55728-685-7

19 18 17 16 15   5 4 3 2 1

Designed by Ellen Beeler
Cover designed by Morgan Bibbs
Cover photos by John Baltz, Russell Cothren, and Mark Reynolds

∞ The paper used in this publication meets the minimum requirements of the American National Standard for Permanence of Paper for Printed Library Materials Z39.48-1984.

Library of Congress Control Number: 2015936352

Contents

Part I Foundations and Scholar Development

Part II Advisors on the Process

Foreword

The National Association of Fellowships Advisors (NAFA) is distinctive in the diverse identities of its membership. Because universities have only recently created fellowships offices or designated individuals as fellowships advisors, there is great variability in where those offices and individuals are located. Fellowships advisors are in honor colleges, dean's or provost's offices, student affairs, career centers, study-abroad programs, and admissions or financial aid offices. For most NAFA members, fellowship and scholarship advising is one of multiple roles they play in the university. Some are faculty members who spend most of their time engaging in teaching and research. Others staff advising centers, guiding students on things like pre–health careers, international study, and postgraduate study as well as fellowships. Still others direct undergraduate research programs or manage honors programs. Some fellowships advisors focus on specific students in a university, for example, all undergraduates, only study-abroad students, or primarily graduate students. Some advisors specialize in international fellowships; others are responsible for a broad range of awards. These differences in background and training, place in the university, and the nature of fellowships advising are one of the strengths of NAFA members: they bring to the organization a breadth of experience and a variety of expertise.

NAFA continues to grow. At the 2013 conference in Atlanta, there were 363 registrants and participants (including invited speakers) from 281 universities or organizations. In addition to representatives from colleges and universities, participants included 39 representatives of fellowship organizations and 15 from British universities. The new advisor workshop was the largest (with 114 participants) NAFA has hosted. NAFA conferences involve long days, and most participants attend *every* session. The 2013 conference was no different—participants spent days of intense focus on scholarship advising, from early in the morning to late evening. The

Intercontinental Hotel hosted the conference, providing excellent places to have conversations, windows that gave appealing glimpses of the outside world between sessions, and an abundance of good food. (Many feared coming to Atlanta in July, but the weather cooperated by being unusually cool and raining only once.)

The 2013 conference marked the end of an era for NAFA, as John Richardson stepped down as treasurer, a position he has held since NAFA's founding. Though John is no longer treasurer, I am happy to say that he has remained involved with NAFA since his retirement. We have not yet had to give up his energy, historic knowledge, and commitment to fellowships advising.

The conference theme for the seventh biennial conference in Atlanta was "Focusing on the Scholar in Scholarship," and many sessions at the conference highlighted the varied ways in which scholarship is supported by fellowships advising. There were sessions for advisors on collaborations with undergraduate research programs and on strategies for involving faculty, graduate students, and other staff in fellowships advising. Because of the diversity in NAFA, the biennial conference can allow advisors working in a specific type of institution or with a certain kind of student to reconnect with others doing the same. In 2013, there were sessions designed for fellowships advisors working with graduate students and a roundtable to connect those advisors. NAFA was happy to welcome to the conference fellowship organizations that have rarely attended NAFA conferences in the past, such as the National Science Foundation, the National Institutes of Health, and the Social Science Research Council.

Highlights of the conference included two sessions about undocumented students. A group of advisors, including Doug Cutchins (NAFA president, 2011–13) and Alicia Hayes (NAFA secretary), have been involved for some time in educating others about the difficulties these students face. They organized two sessions involving Kathy Gin and Jose Arreola from Educators for Fair Consideration (E4FC) and Deisy Del Real, a Grinnell alumna and Soros fellow who has been an activist on this issue. A presentation in the plenary session was followed by a working session on how to be an ally and advisor for undocumented students.

Elizabeth Ambos, the executive director of the Council on Undergraduate Research, gave a talk titled "Students as Scholars." She discussed the growth of research experiences for undergraduates, both in science fields, where it has traditionally been available, and in the social sciences and humanities, where an expansion of those opportunities is more recent. The growth of these programs means that undergraduates in more fields can bring to fellowship applications significant experience producing new scholarship. For fellowships advisors, she advocated working closely with those involved in undergraduate research and urged them to be advocates for research on their own campuses. Though some national funding supports undergraduate research in the natural and social sciences, opportunities in the humanities and arts are mostly limited to students' home campuses.

Though many conference participants were new advisors, veteran advisors make up the majority of conference participants, and different opportunities are useful to more experienced advisors. In 2013, a pre-conference workshop for this group focused on the Truman Scholarship, similar in some respects to the 2011 reading session hosted by the Udall Scholarship. This was organized to replicate Truman reading sessions to select finalists and was designed to help advisors better understand what happens to their applications once they are released. Tara Yglesias organized and offered this session, despite her concern that advisors would learn nothing from the exercise (to quote from her instructions "I Cannot Guarantee an Epiphany—Individual Results May Vary"). For participants, the experience gave a good understanding of how difficult the process is to choose finalists from among excellent candidates who have already been vetted by their universities. Though few advisors probably experienced an epiphany, most agreed that they learned a great deal about the selection process from the experience. Special thanks go to her and to the Truman Foundation, who have been longtime supporters of NAFA.

The biennial national conferences provide an opportunity to gather as a community to think about our larger goals, but between the biennial conferences, the NAFA board also works hard for NAFA members. NAFA is an organization that some misunderstand. For advisors, students succeed if the application process allows them to grow as individuals and to better understand themselves and their goals—whether or not students are awarded a scholarship. Some, however, are convinced that fellowships advising is about erasing a student's voice rather than helping the student find it. I am proud of the work that the current NAFA board has undertaken—both in public and private—to advocate for NAFA's philosophy and to challenge any mistaken ideas about our work.

This volume of essays continues the conversations that grew out of the biennial conference. Advisors and foundations, from various perspectives, examine the impact of fellowships advising, look at how advisors connect with students, and outline the best practices for the profession.

Joanne Brzinski
Emory University
NAFA President, 2013–15

Acknowledgments

The National Association of Fellowships Advisors (NAFA) held its seventh biennial conference in Atlanta in July 2013. Many of the essays included in this volume grew out of the discussions held there. The conference could not have taken place and these proceedings would not exist without the hard work of a significant number of people. Doug Cutchins (Grinnell College) was president of NAFA at the time of the conference and provided oversight for the organization for the two years previous to the Atlanta gathering. Joanne Brzinski (Emory University) was the vice president when the conference occurred and assumed the role of president at the conference's end. The vice president is the main person responsible for organizing the event, which includes inviting speakers, calling for papers, negotiating with hotels, coordinating panels, and carrying out a long list of other tasks. Joanne Brzinski had significant help from her planning committee: Lyn Fulton-John (Vanderbilt University), Dana Kuchem (The Ohio State University), Sue Nichols (Texas A&M University–Kingsville), Ricki Shine (Clemson University), and Jeff Wing (Virginia Commonwealth University). John Richardson (University of Louisville), NAFA treasurer, and Alicia Hayes (University of California, Berkeley), who was NAFA secretary, were also instrumental in making the event happen. NAFA board members from 2011–13 all contributed significantly to the conference: Laura Damuth (University of Nebraska–Lincoln), David Schug (University of Illinois at Urbana-Champaign), Susan Whitbourne (University of Massachusetts–Amherst), Julia Goldberg (Lafayette College), Belinda Redden (University of Rochester), Lyn Fulton-John (Vanderbilt University), Dana Kuchem (The Ohio State University), Tony Cashman (College of the Holy Cross), Luke Green (Seattle University), and Kyle Mox (University of Chicago). Sue Sharp (IIE/Boren) served as the foundation representative, and Tara Yglesias (Truman Scholarship Foundation) and Nicole Gelfert (University of Central Florida) were the communications directors.

Other conference planners and special contributors include Nour El-Kebbi (Emory University), Megan Friddle (Emory University), Kim Benard (Massachusetts Institute of Technology), Bob Graalman (Oklahoma State University), Karen Weber (University of Houston), Babs Wise (Duke University), Monique Bourque (Willamette University), Joan Echols (American University), Beth Fiori (Cornell University), Scott Henderson (Furman University), Lisa Kooperman (Vassar College), Ruth Mendum (Pennsylvania State University), Mona Pitre-Collins (University of Washington), Linna Place (University of Missouri–Kansas City), Judy Zang (University of Pittsburgh), Mary Denyer (Marshall Aid Commemoration Commission), Robin Chang (University of Washington), Laura Neidert (Hampden-Sydney College), Kefryn Reese (University of Miami–Coral Gables), Elizabeth Colucci (State University of New York at Buffalo), Karna Walter (University of Arizona), Jane Curlin (Udall Foundation), Paula Randler (Udall Foundation), Denise Gagnon (Amherst College), Katya King (Williams College), Joan Echols (American University), Brian Souders (University of Maryland, Baltimore County), and all who presented at the conference.

The conference was sponsored by the Emory Office for Undergraduate Education, the Emory Office of International Affairs, and Emory College Computing. Printing was done by Emory Document Services.

The active participation of foundations during national and regional conferences is critical to the continued success of NAFA in providing advisors with accurate and appropriate information to share with their students. The foundation representatives who were particularly unstinting in their contribution to the Atlanta conference include Jane Curlin (Udall Foundation), Paula Randler (Udall Foundation), Leslie Root (Critical Languages Scholarship Program), Gisele Muller-Parker (National Science Foundation Grant), Frank Gilmore (Goldwater Scholarship Foundation), Tara Yglesias (Truman Scholarship Foundation), Andrew Rich (Truman Scholarship Foundation), Brent Drage (Rotary Foundation Fellowships), Cheryl Scott Mouzon (Jack Kent Cooke Foundation), Walter Jackson (Fulbright/IIE), Amra Dumisic (DAAD), Margarita Valencia (National Institute of Mental Health Partnership Programs), Trina Vargo (Mitchell Scholarship Program), Serena Wilson (Mitchell Scholarship Program),

Jim Smith (Gates Cambridge Trust), Ralph Smith (Rhodes Scholarship Trust), Todd Peterson (Rhodes Scholarship Trust), Katharine Wilkinson (Rhodes Scholarship Trust), Mary Denyer (Marshall Aid Commemoration Commission), Mary Edgerton (Marshall Aid Commemoration Commission), Annabelle Malins (Marshall Aid Commemoration Commission), Amy Stursberg (Schwarzman Scholars Program), Thomas Christensen (Schwarzman Scholars Program), Patricia Scroggs (Rangel International Affairs Program), Daniella Sarnoff (Social Science Research Council), Shawna Hurley (Gilman Scholarship Program), Li Ling (Luce Scholars Program), Nicole Susco (Cultural Vistas), Philip Ugelow (Humanity in Action Fellowship), Tom Parkinson (Beinecke Scholarship/The Sperry Fund), and Yulian Ramos (Soros Foundation).

Keynote speaker Elizabeth L. Ambos, PhD, the executive officer for the Council on Undergraduate Research (CUR), helped emphasize the conference theme, "Focusing on the Scholar in the Scholarship Process." We were also very pleased to be joined by leaders of Educators for Fair Consideration (E4FC), including Katherine Gin, Jose Arreola, and Deisy Del Real, who spoke of the necessity of outreach to undocumented students in the scholarship advising process.

Tara Yglesias and Andrew Rich, from the Truman Scholarship Foundation, and their colleagues Andy Kirk, Whitney Shufelt, and Tonji Wade, organized and led a preconference workshop on the Truman Scholarship, allowing NAFA members to experience what it means to serve on a selection committee. Joanne Brzinski, Alicia Hayes, and Liz Veatch (American Councils for International Education) assisted them in this endeavor.

For this volume of essays, special thanks goes to the NAFA Publications Board, especially cochairs Lisa Kooperman (Vassar College) and Mona Pitre-Collins (University of Washington), and the authors, whose energetic work in their offices and in their writing created both interesting and helpful essays to share with NAFA members, faculty mentors, and students.

Thanks to staff members at New York University Abu Dhabi, who were highly supportive of this work, especially the Career Development Center's Hazel Raja (assistant dean of students and director of Career Development Center), Zach Troia (preprofessional services coordinator), and Tracey Corcoran (administrative coordinator); the Campus Life Division's David Tinagero (associate vice chancellor of student affairs and dean of students) and Donna Eddleman (deputy dean of students); and university leadership including President John Sexton, Linda Mills (vice chancellor for Global Programs and University Life), and Al Bloom (vice chancellor, NYU Abu Dhabi).

Thanks go as well to the staff of Enrollment Services at the University of Arkansas and to the Office of Nationally Competitive Awards in particular. Without their support this edition would simply not be possible. Jeremy Burns (associate director) and Jonathan Langley (assistant director) provided excellent proofreading help, and Dianna Winters-Lewis (director of creative design, Enrollment Services) assisted with graph design. Thanks also go to Morgan Bibbs (assistant director of creative design for Enrollment Services) who designed a lovely cover. The ongoing support of Chancellor G. David Gearhart, Provost Sharon Gaber, Dean Tom Smith of the College of Education and Health Professions, and Ketevan Mamiseishvili (department chair of Rehabilitation, Human Resources, and Communication Disorders) has also helped make this publication possible as have the efforts of the University of Arkansas Press: Mike Bieker (director); Brian King (director of Editing, Design, and Production); David Scott Cunningham (acquisitions editor); and Melissa King (director of Marketing).

Finally, we again want to specially thank John Richardson, who retired as NAFA's first and only treasurer at the Atlanta conference, and who was recognized at the closing banquet for his years of capable, unwavering, good-natured work for the organization. From conference registrations to membership to negotiations with hotels to overseas trips, John had a hand in every major (and minor) NAFA initiative since its birth in 1999. The organization would not be the same without his dedication.

ALL BEFORE THEM

Introduction

Students applying for nationally and internationally competitive scholarships and fellowships usually have an accomplished past, are actively engaged in their discipline and in their communities, and possess a strong sense of direction for the future. They are not fuzzy-cheeked beginners—in this our title's Miltonic reference is at least temporally misleading—but the world is all before them, and they stand at pivotal thresholds, faced with a bewildering array of professional opportunities. They have every motive to make themselves as well informed as possible while weighing life-shaping decisions. This collection of essays aims to assist advisors, faculty mentors, and students in that process.

All before Them: Student Opportunities and Nationally Competitive Fellowships is divided into three sections. The first includes important information from foundations. The second offers suggestions from experienced advisors and faculty on successful approaches to engaging students in the process. The third focuses on tools advisors can use to improve the services they provide; the topics here range from specific kinds of technology, to ePortfolios, to assessment. Robert Garris, the global director of admissions for the Schwarzman Scholars, provides the first essay in the collection, offering important information from one of NAFA's newest foundation members. In "Schwarzman Scholars: Building a Global Network of China-Savvy Leaders," Garris outlines a remarkable new opportunity for students whose fields of study connect them to China. According to Garris, the goal is to have thousands of Schwarzman Scholars and key leaders working together across the globe by 2050. This is an amazing vision, and fellowships advisors will want to follow the progress of the program closely. Stephen Schwarzman, using the Rhodes Scholarship as a model, has involved world leaders to create a scholarship program that will not only provide its recipients with a year at Tsinghua University but will also make them part of a lifetime community of world leaders. The advisory board itself sets the tone with former secretaries of state, prime ministers, and university presidents as well as key corporate and intellectual leaders.

Working with Tsinghua University president Jining Chen and with architect Robert Stern, Schwarzman is building a new Schwarzman College for these scholars on the Tsinghua campus. He has been aided by institutions from across the globe to develop application and selection procedures that will lead to the selection of exceptional individuals with the potential to become world leaders. Students applying for the scholarship will also be applying for the college, with the first cohort set to arrive on campus in 2016. The admissions and scholarship selection processes promise to be rigorous, and Garris provides a glimpse of what the key areas of focus for Schwarzman application reviewers will be. Advisors, students, and foundations alike will read with interest as Garris outlines the future of this remarkable program.

Chapter 2 focuses on the Mitchell Scholarship, a familiar program that has recently embraced a video technology as part of its selection process. As most advisors know, the Mitchell Scholarship (named for former U.S. Senator George Mitchell) selects twelve scholars each year. The rigorous process has one unique feature: a video introduction. This is not a bidirectional interview; no live person is involved at the other end of the camera as there would be in a Skype interview. This is simply a recorded response to a randomly delivered set of questions being offered for the students to address. In her essay "The Mitchell Video: First Impressions," Serena Wilson discusses the mechanics and goals of the video interview. She stresses one very important message for students and advisors involved in this process: authenticity matters. Students need to be themselves if they want to be successful.

The first section's third and final chapter is from Tara Yglesias at the Truman Foundation. Yglesias has provided essays for various NAFA volumes in the past, including one about what leadership means in connection with the Truman Scholarship application and one that is a guide for students who are selected for interview. Both essays ("Non Ducor, Duco: Leadership and the Truman Scholarship Application," and "Enough about Me, What Do You Think about Me? Surviving the Truman Interview") provide a lively and immensely informative discussion of key aspects of the Truman application process, and both are very helpful advising tools. The essay in this volume, "I Love It When a Grad Plan Comes Together:

Graduate School Advising and the Truman Application," is in that same vein. The title, with its reference to the *A-Team,* hints at prose that will be a pleasure to read. In the essay Yglesias suggests ways to help students think about both the formulation and the articulation of graduate school plans. In describing how Truman Scholarship reviewers read applications, she provides insights about what general advice is important for students as they consider and describe their academic plans. In a lighthearted but ultimately serious discussion, Yglesias also provides a look at where students often go wrong.

The second section includes four essays focusing on the advisor at work. Two of the essays concentrate on the personal statement, the third on expanding opportunities by adding additional scholarships to the advisor's repertoire, and the fourth on effective scholarship recruitment. Chapter 4, in an essay titled simply "The Personal Statement," offers Jenni Quilter's thoughtful look at the advisor's sometime unintended but always shaping effect on a student's writing. The changes in the Rhodes policy on its personal statement—that no one may review or edit it other than the student—is at the heart of her reflections. This change sparked a heated debate among NAFA members, who energetically and sometimes vocally took sides on the issue. Quilter, herself a Rhodes Scholar, who now directs New York University's fellowships office and works in the Expository Writing Program, acknowledges that most writing in the real world takes place with multiple reviewers providing input to authors, who can then choose whether to take advice, which is always amply given. She questions whether students at the application stage in their lives have the same ability to resist influence. Her essay provides a thoughtful examination of the process and gives insight from an applicant-turned-advisor's point of view. For some advisors who take exception to the Rhodes decision, this essay may help make it more comprehensible.

Quilter's essay is followed by another perspective on the personal statement writing process. Lowell Frye, a rhetoric and humanities professor at Hampden-Sydney College, makes clear in chapter 5 he is not writing a *how-to* essay in his "Exploring One's Life for Others: Reflections on Writing the Personal Statement," but is instead looking at why students find the personal statement so difficult to write, and in doing so, he provides helpful advice on encouraging students to think productively about their own experiences: "Fellowship advisors cannot teach students to be self-aware any more than we can achieve for them excellence in and out of the classroom. But we can ask them questions, press for elaboration, encourage them to reach beyond the tried-and-true, the formulaic. We can help them to identify and articulate the strengths they harbor, sometimes without knowing it."

Doug Cutchins, an experienced advisor who spent the first fifteen years of his career at Grinnell College, decided last year to make a major change in his professional life. He took a newly created fellowships advisor position at New York University Abu Dhabi. This transition offered him the opportunity to start again, reviewing what he knew about advising and what he still needed to learn, given his new environment and the resources available to him. The title of his essay (chapter 6) shares that examination: "Bring Something Old, Learn Something New, Borrow a Lot, and Conduct an Analytical Review." What his essay brings home to advisors, who may be less willing to uproot themselves so dramatically, is that it is important to routinely "shake up routines" and take a fresh look at the ways their offices operate. Learning something new is a central message in this essay, and Cutchins outlines an approach for doing so. He also helps jump-start that learning for advisors by providing four scholarships opportunities that may not be on every institution's list to promote. Advisors frequently encourage students to stretch beyond what is comfortable and to embrace new challenges. Cutchins encourages advisors to do the same.

Connecting the right student with the right scholarship is a key element in the fellowships advising process. In "Workshops That Attract and Engage Students" (chapter 7), Monique Bourque (Willamette University), Laura Cotton (University of Dayton), and Becky Mentzer (Illinois State University) provide innovative ways for advisors to reach out to and connect competitive students with awards that fit well with their career goals. High-achieving students tend to have full calendars. They need to be clear why a scholarship application (that can take in some cases more than thirty hours to complete) is an appropriate use of the limited time they have available. Traditional informational meetings may not always be the best method (though it is certainly the easiest and most tempting) to attract students who could benefit from and be competitive for particular scholarships. In this essay, the authors provide alternative approaches.

The Advisor Toolkit section of the collection of essays has more to do with the information and technology aspects of advising. The four essays look at foundational elements that can help support what advisors do. The first essay provides a review of the various forms of technologies that advisors have available to them. But as the title "More Connected? Implications of Information and Communication Technology for Fellowships Advising" makes clear, the technologies that advisors choose to employ can shape their interaction with students more than intended. The benefits of the uses of technology are straightforward: outreach to more students, connecting in familiar venues that will encourage response, assisting or including those abroad, ease in data collection and production of materials, and tools for assessment. Though she does not intend her list to be exhaustive, Jennifer Gerz-Escandón provides a wealth of information in chapter 8 about the types and categories of technology that advisors could or do use. But the question remains: Are advisors really more connected? The answer seems to be yes at times and no at others. Gerz-Escandón looks at some of the downsides of technology in our lives but also provides an optimistic view of how advisors can use technology effectively to expand, but not replace, the human side of the advising effort.

In chapter 9, Karen Weber provides an interesting look at harnessing students' drive to share information about themselves through social media and put it to academic and professional use through ePortfolios. The University of Houston's Honors College has developed an ePortfolio program, which Weber directs. Such programs are gaining in popularity on campuses across the country and provide "a competency-based tool for students to demonstrate their learning and career readiness to employers, graduate school admissions committees, and even one day perhaps to scholarship foundations." Houston even offers a one-hour ePortfolio course. Weber provides examples of effective student ePortfolios and recommends them as a possible tool for fellowships advisors as a means to encourage students to be reflective about their academic and service experiences and to connect their understanding of those experiences with their future goals. Such a tool could assist students as they put their accomplishments into perspective, block out a future career path, and articulate those plans in competitive scholarship applications.

Effectively identifying students who will be competitive for awards is the subject of chapter 10, "Advanced Placement as a Tool for Scholarship and Fellowship Advisors." Advisors often work with registrar's offices to secure names and email addresses of students with high grade point averages in various fields of study in order to invite these students to various information meetings or personal appointments about scholarships. Suzanne McCray (University of Arkansas) suggests in this essay that advisors also consider including AP and IB scores in their requests as well. Students who score well on these exams—and most institutions in NAFA give at least some credit for AP and IB work—often are able to embrace the kinds of extracurricular activities (research, service, student abroad, internships) that will enhance their educational experiences and increase the likelihood that they will be competitive (for those who also have strong academic performances) for the nationally competitive awards in their fields. This may be most helpful to public institutions, especially land grant universities, that award significant credit and that may have a broad mix of student preparedness at the institution.

Chapter 11, the final chapter of the advising tools section and the book, addresses the need for assessment. Monique Bourque (Willamette University), Julia Goldberg (Lafayette College), and Tim Parshall (University of Missouri–Columbia) tackle the problem in "How Am I Doing and How Do I Know? Fellowships and Meaningful Assessment." While assessment is important for both foundations and for advising offices, this essay focuses on the latter group. The authors stress that assessment for such offices has to be about more than simply counting up the number of winners and honorable mentions and benchmarking it against other institutions, if advisors take seriously the charge (and want to encourage administrators at their institutions to understand) that their purposes go "beyond winning." Assessment can be critically important to securing additional funding, for successful hiring requests, and to encourage support from central and upper administration at the institution. But knowing it is important and designing an effective assessment approach can be very different things. This essay provides a helpful approach to developing an effective assessment process. The "Survey of the Profession" found in appendix B can assist advisors when making institutional comparisons.

The number of the advisors who focus on nationally and internationally competitive awards is growing. The NAFA listserv has more than seven hundred participants, and the number of institutional members in the organization is over four hundred. Advisors must simultaneously keep abreast of new scholarship opportunities, find effective ways to communicate information to qualified students, advise students appropriately, develop a campus infrastructure that engages faculty and administrators, learn new technologies to assist with various aspects of recruitment and advising, define and assess success for the office, and plan strategically. The work is both interesting and complex. The essays in this volume are intended to provide advisors with additional tools to help expand opportunities for exceptional, high-achieving students, who have all before them.

Part I

Foundations and Scholar Development

1

Schwarzman Scholars
Building a Global Network of China-Savvy Leaders

ROBERT GARRIS

Robert Garris is the Global Director of Admissions for Schwarzman Scholars and has built innovative international programs at universities and foundations for more than fifteen years. Prior to joining Schwarzman Scholars, he served as a managing director at the Rockefeller Foundation, developing the Bellagio Center conference and international fellows programs into a major global convening site addressing critical global issues. Garris spent eight years at Columbia University's School of International and Public Affairs (SIPA). As senior associate dean, he coordinated administrative, student, and academic affairs on behalf of the dean. He managed the university's launch of a Global Center in Beijing and led efforts to build a network of partner institutions in Europe, Asia, and Latin America. He also served as the director of Admissions and Student Affairs at Johns Hopkins University School of Advanced International Studies. Garris received his PhD in European history from the University of North Carolina, where he specialized in immigration and urban policy.

By the middle of this century, a global network of ten thousand influential women and men, holding leadership positions in business, government, and civil society around the world, will work together to promote a more peaceful and prosperous world. They will be more effective in their work because Schwarzman Scholars will have given them firsthand knowledge of China and the role it plays in global trends, and will have linked them to each other as a mutually supporting network for creating positive change in the world. Moving this vision forward from Stephen A. Schwarzman's initial inspiration is a complex process relying on the advice, insights, and energy of partners ranging from political leaders in China and academic leaders at Tsinghua University to political, academic, business, and youth leaders from around the world.

The Inspiration

Schwarzman recognizes that the twenty-first century requires a new kind of leadership, based in a truly global network reflecting emerging centers of power and in firsthand experience of the remarkable influence that China has on global trends. Challenges and solutions for human prosperity and well-being are emerging from all corners of the planet, but in almost all cases, China is playing a central role. Rapidly changing global markets, innovations in renewable energy, financial volatility, international diplomacy, and population stresses on the planet's resources—the next generation of leaders will need to understand how these trends and many more are being shaped by China. Schwarzman admires how the Rhodes Scholarship has built generations of leaders by educating them early in their careers and by connecting them to each other as a global cohort. Building on that model, but with a twenty-first-century focus on China, he has partnered with the leadership of one of China's top educational institutions, Tsinghua University, and with academic, political, and business leaders from around the world, to develop a new fellowship, the Schwarzman Scholars. By midcentury, Schwarzman Scholars will be a worldwide network of leaders of corporations, governments, and nonprofit organizations, all more effective in their efforts through their knowledge of China and their connections to each other.

Executing the Vision

In 2013, Schwarzman and Tsinghua University's President Jining Chen agreed to create Schwarzman College, which will offer a one-year master's degree in public policy, international studies, or business and economics. The college will serve as the home for Schwarzman Scholars during their year at Tsinghua. Advancing from that initial vision and agreement to the opening day for the first class, on July 5, 2016, is a globally collaborative effort. An international advisory board—consisting of global political and academic leaders including Condoleezza Rice, Tony Blair, Richard Levin, and Robert Rubin—provides high-level support and advice. An academic advisory council, composed of distinguished academics from Asia, North America, and Europe, is working closely with Schwarzman Scholars' leadership and Tsinghua University faculty to build out the curriculum and programming, bringing diverse international perspectives and experience to the creation of a truly global educational effort. The design of a highly competitive admissions program has similarly benefited from the input of the advisory council, fellowships advisors from around the world, graduate admissions professionals, and the Rhodes Trust. This admissions process will draw on local and regional experts to assess and interview candidates and will be driven by a global set of admissions standards, with final selections determined by a small global committee.

World-renowned architect Robert A. M. Stern is leading the construction of Schwarzman College. The college is a state-of-the-art facility with living, study, and social spaces that promote interaction among students and faculty and welcome visitors from the rest of the Tsinghua campus and the world. The college, to be completed in fall of 2015, will use the most advanced instructional technologies and provide students, faculty, and guests with the highest-quality living, learning, health, and environmental facilities available.

The work to execute the Schwarzman Scholars vision continues. In 2015, small international teams of faculty are finalizing syllabi and piloting a core curriculum covering Chinese culture and history, global economics, global international relations, comparative governance, and leadership. Partner graduate schools at Tsinghua University are working with Schwarzman College to ensure that scholars will have robust and flexible options to craft a set of concentration courses reflecting their individual interests in public policy, international studies, or business and economics. The college has already begun recruiting distinguished Tsinghua faculty to the program, and a dynamic schedule of visiting faculty is being crafted, bringing in leading scholars from around the world to teach at Schwarzman College. In some instances visitors will co-teach with Tsinghua faculty; sometimes they will teach their own classes, but in all cases, visitors and Tsinghua faculty will work together to ensure Schwarzman Scholars are exposed to diverse perspectives on how China is changing and how it is driving change in the world.

The admissions team will finish recruiting and training expert interviewers and readers around the world by midsummer, building them into a global team focused on identifying scholars with outstanding leadership potential combined with academic excellence. In October and November, regional selection panels, composed of academics and other business and political experts, will begin their work to choose the first cohort of Schwarzman Scholars.

In Beijing, public, private, and nonprofit organizations will take on Schwarzman Scholars as interns each spring, providing them with hands-on experience working in leading Chinese and international entities based in Beijing. Senior-level figures are also agreeing to serve as mentors for Schwarzman Scholars, helping them understand their fields in China and connecting them to other leading professional figures. Intensive, deep-dive study tours—a hallmark of the Schwarzman Scholars experience—will also be designed and piloted in 2015. These tours, arranged in small groups, will give scholars the opportunity to intensively examine a critical issue in contemporary China in one region, away from Beijing and Shanghai, deepening their understanding of the country and expanding even further the professional networks they will carry with them for the rest of their careers. This combination of internships, mentorships, and intensive study tours will build on the leadership themes in the curriculum to accelerate the scholars' exploration of their own approaches to leadership and their understanding of their host country.

Defining Leadership

Given that this young cohort of students, with a maximum age of twenty-eight, will have only just begun to explore their leadership styles and experiences, the program's selection process will focus on a set of personal traits that are the foundation of future success as leaders. Schwarzman Scholars must demonstrate three key characteristics that define the program's understanding of leadership, and the program will also invite applicants to identify other characteristics that have shaped their personal approaches to leadership:

- Leadership: the ability to conceptualize, articulate, and implement new approaches to existing conditions, with determination, energy, and adaptability to drive change despite obstacles. A leader needs the ability to inspire others to help make change happen. The program asserts that leadership can be demonstrated through many contexts and fields: political, social, business, the arts, and beyond.
- Intellect: achievements demonstrated through outstanding performance in academic endeavors. A strong intellect is the foundation of effective leadership and will be essential for success in the academic program at Tsinghua.
- Character: personal values and integrity that inspire trust among others and drive the young leader's decision making.

Identifying a globally and professionally diverse cohort of young people with leadership potential will require the insights of advisors, readers, and interviewers from around the world. We will rely on faculty, advisors, mentors, and eventually alumni to spot candidates who have the right combination of academic excellence, the personal characteristics necessary for leadership, and the energy and drive to act on that potential. On campuses, in businesses, in government offices around the world, there are senior figures who are in the right position to know who among their younger colleagues or students seems to have the skills and inclination to take on leadership positions, and Schwarzman Scholars will rely on a network of these advisors and mentors to direct Schwarzman Scholars our way.

In choosing among the many well-qualified candidates who will apply, we will also rely on local and regional knowledge to bring the most talented applicants to the top of the pool. Reading and interviewing committees will be constructed on a regional basis, so that we can benefit from critical cultural and social insights to understand how academic talent and leadership potential manifest themselves in different university and professional contexts. Those committees will read applications, drawing on the candidates' academic credentials, essays that highlight their leadership potential and aspirations, and reference letters. The application will also solicit input from universities for those candidates who are still undergraduates. University assessment forms will confirm that students are on track to graduate the following year and will ask for other brief factual insights that may not be reflected in the academic record or faculty reference letters. Based on these insights, the reading committees will identify a semifinalist list of several hundred candidates to be invited to regional interviews in North America, South America, Europe, and Asia. Those regional interviews will test the candidates' intellectual agility, their vision for the future, their ability to inspire others, and their character, in group and individual formats, to generate recommendations for the final selection committee. That small committee, based on Schwarzman Scholars staff and faculty from New York and Beijing, will then curate a global and professional mix across the regions, creating the high-capacity talent pool and diverse perspectives that will be essential to the Schwarzman College learning environment.

This emphasis on leadership goes beyond the application process. It informs the core curriculum, the internships and study tours, and the long-term vision for Schwarzman Scholars alumni. Those who join the program as Schwarzman Scholars take on a commitment that extends far beyond their year in China. They are committed to taking on leadership positions in their fields, to working collaboratively as a global cohort, and to promoting the long-term vision of a more peaceful and prosperous world. Empowered by their year at Tsinghua and their lifelong engagement with each other, they will be unlike any network of leaders the world has seen before.

2

The Mitchell Video
First Impressions

SERENA WILSON

*Serena **Williams** is the director of the Mitchell Scholarship, a program of the US-Ireland Alliance. For several years, Wilson served as the president of Friends of Riverbend Park in Great Falls, Virginia. An environmental lawyer by trade, Wilson was appointed by President Clinton to the Joint Public Advisory Committee for the North American Agreement on Environmental Cooperation under NAFTA. Prior to that she served at the Environmental Protection Agency as the coordinator for trade and environment policy. She was also chief of the Biodiversity Team in the Office of Protected Resources for the National Marine Fisheries Service, and an international trade specialist at the U.S. Department of Commerce. She taught environmental law at American University, worked in a law firm, and led programs in several rain forests around the world. She graduated magna cum laude from the University of Connecticut with a BS in biochemistry and BA in German. She also holds a JD from the Washington College of Law.*

The Mitchell Scholarship entered new territory in 2012 when it added a video interview component to its application process. Evaluating candidates with a video interview was a groundbreaking step for competitive scholarships, which most likely made advisors and candidates alike very nervous. What is the purpose of this video interview? What exactly is the Mitchell Scholarship Program trying to learn about the candidate? How does the process work? I will address these questions here, but I caution advisors that in reading this, do not hope to find the ideal formula for a successful video interview. There really is not one. It is our goal to make sure that there is not one.

First, understanding the nature of the Mitchell Scholarship Program is important for gaining a full appreciation for why we want to meet scholarship candidates in a few different scenarios before choosing finalists. This scholarship is named to honor former U.S. Senator George Mitchell's pivotal contribution to the Northern Ireland peace process and is designed to introduce and connect generations of future American leaders to the island of Ireland. Up to twelve Mitchell Scholars between the ages of eighteen and thirty are chosen annually for one year of postgraduate study in any discipline offered by institutions of higher learning in Ireland and Northern Ireland. The Mitchell Scholarship Program provides tuition, accommodation, and a stipend for living expenses and travel.

The scholarship is a prestigious award, and the application process is very competitive. Applicants have just under a 4 percent chance of winning and are judged on three criteria: academic excellence, leadership, and a sustained commitment to public service. One universally appreciated element of our program is that the scholars in each Mitchell class participate together in organized events throughout the Mitchell year.

Mitchell Scholars travel together and congregate with their Mitchell class often, and they are part of the Mitchell Scholarship community for life. During the scholarship year, the program staff travels to Ireland or Northern Ireland three times to gather the scholars for orientation, a midyear retreat, and a commencement weekend. Scholars also have an option to spend Thanksgiving together at an Irish family's home. These gatherings entail travel around the island of Ireland and meetings with many prominent people, so that the scholars are often put in a position of acting as ambassadors for the program and for the United States.

Following their Mitchell year, each scholar is a member of the alumni community and is invited to Mitchell events in the area in which they live, and, we hope, is actively part of the engine that runs the Mitchell Scholarship Program. There are currently 170 Mitchell Scholars, including the class in Ireland for the 2014–15 academic year.

The video interview became part of our process after thirteen years of experience in selecting scholars without it. What we were seeing in the selection process at that point was a steady increase in formulaic applications, where candidates were no longer presenting themselves as themselves but instead presenting to us what they thought we wanted to see. When it came to the semifinal interviews, we were finding that the candidates we met often did not match up with the candidates on paper.

This concept of trying to define the parameters of a model Mitchell Scholar is baffling. The parameters are not what is baffling, but the idea that people seek a model at all. To someone who knows many of the Mitchell Scholars, it is clear that they are diverse in every sense of the word—their interests, schools, U.S. state of origin, race, age, gender, religion, sexual orientation, and so on.

Each scholar chosen during the selection process is more than just a person handed funds to study abroad. Each scholar is joining a diverse community of Mitchell Scholars to which they will add their unique backgrounds, interests, expertise, and future goals. There is no formula. Each scholar will contribute to the Mitchell class and all of the programs in which that class participates, and then become part of the larger Mitchell community of people advising and networking with each other to contribute to their communities, the country, and the United States–Ireland relationship.

Understanding what the Mitchell Scholarship Program expects of our scholars may help advisors better understand the purpose of the video interview. The US-Ireland Alliance sees each Mitchell Scholar as a life-long part of the organization, so we desire to really know the finalists as individuals and to understand how they will fit into our community. Also, scholars need to be able to effectively present an idea in order to represent our program on the island of Ireland or discuss the program at U.S. universities. We find it beneficial to see each applicant in many different situations rather than just seeing the person who is carefully presented on paper or prepped for an interview.

The video interview component of the Mitchell application brings an element of improvisation into the process. Our purpose is simple: we want to get to know the candidates better. For those unfamiliar with the video interview process, details of how it works may be helpful. After an applicant submits his or her written application, the Mitchell Scholarship director must deem that application complete. All applicants who submit completed applications before the application period closes will proceed to the video interview.

The Irish company Sonru, which was listed as one of the world's top technology start-ups in 2010, runs our video process. The Sonru solution is intended to replace the first round of phone or on-site interviews in any recruitment process, and as such is increasingly used by major companies in their talent acquisition searches. Due to this increased use, practice with the online video interview process is useful to all Mitchell candidates, as they may one day use it in the marketplace. A new service offered starting in 2014 is the option for applicants to conduct the interview using Android phones or iPhones, as long as the phone has a front-facing camera.

Each candidate receives an email at a designated time, usually the day following the close of the application process. This email has written instructions for the video portion of the application and the link for starting the interview process. Sonru provides for a practice session, enabling all applicants to test their video connections for video and sound quality. There is no limit on how many times an applicant can run through the practice exercise. If a candidate has trouble with either video or sound quality, he or she can contact Sonru Support, who are on call 24/7 and should answer within an hour no matter where in world the applicant is recording.

Each year, candidates living in remote corners of the world apply for a Mitchell Scholarship. For these people, finding a reliable Internet connection is an added complication for the video component. Unfortunately, we cannot exempt anyone from the video interview due to hardship, so the key for these applicants is planning. Everyone knows that the video interview is a requirement well in advance, and thus should have a plan for finding a reliable Internet connection, whether that be in a school, café, government building, or library, or at the dock three villages over. For those needing to seek out a special Internet connection, we recommend that candidates start this process immediately, in case that reliable connection is not so reliable and it takes the applicant a few tries. The candidate should be prepared in case the power goes out during the first attempt. The applicants have seventy-two hours to complete the video interview, although the interview itself takes less than ten minutes. We have yet to have any major issues with this requirement; if there is a problem that is not the fault of the candidate, we will work with the candidate to resolve it.

Once the Internet connection is established and the practice sessions have resulted in good video quality, the applicant is ready to start the interview. The interview consists of three questions randomly chosen from a list of questions provided by the Mitchell program. There is also a fourth time slot of two minutes, allowing the interviewee to add any other information or clarification he or she finds necessary. These two minutes should not be used to thank the Mitchell program staff for giving the applicant the opportunity to interview. If the applicant has nothing new to add to their interview, it is best to pass on this fourth question. A reviewer can be equally impressed by an applicant who knows when to stop talking as by one who recognizes a useful point to make.

The questions are randomized. The first year that we used the video interviews, we gave all three hundred or so applicants the same three questions. In this era of information sharing, the candidates who completed the video interview on the first available day decided to share the questions with their competitors who had not yet interviewed. While we do not understand why anyone would do this, the situation created an unfair advantage for those who were scheduled later in the process. It also undermined our desire to see an interviewee in an improvisational scenario. The point is not to prepare for this part of the process.

The second year, we had a series of questions, and each interviewee received a random set of three questions. In giving random questions, we wanted to make the process fair and create a level playing field. We hoped to have the interviewee talk about a random subject, allowing us to learn something new about the applicant. Unfortunately, no matter what question was asked, some applicants veered into a stock speech about themselves and why they should be Mitchell Scholars. This prepared response to random questions is not the response we are seeking.

Each question specifies the allotted amount of time that the person has to prepare an answer, usually around thirty seconds, and then to answer that question, which is one, two, or three minutes. Once the time is reached, the camera shuts off, and the applicant can request the next question. The applicant should finish each question within the requested time, as it is better to finish early than to be cut off.

Since no one is present but the applicant and a video program, there are no follow-up questions. The answers are recorded. We attach the video to the bottom of the candidate's application. When a person evaluating a candidate opens the application, the video is viewed as part of the application. We advise our readers to evaluate the written material first and then watch the video.

A few people get caught in a pitfall caused by time zones. All Mitchell Scholarship deadlines are Eastern Standard Time (EST) and are firm. If the video component closes at 5:00 p.m. EST and an applicant is in Dallas trying to answer a question at 4:55 p.m., he missed the deadline and will not be allowed to complete the video interview. An applicant must be organized enough to submit an application on time, organize the recommenders to submit on time, and finish the video on time, all of which are part of the selection process. If the applicant cannot meet deadlines, we find this telling, and they self-select themselves out of the process.

The best advice to every applicant hoping for a successful video interview is to "be themselves" and not be so serious that they cannot relax. We are not trying to stump the applicant with trick questions that require research. We are just trying to get to know the applicants through simple questions. The applicant will know the answers.

This video interview component of the selection process may continue to evolve. After two years of using the videos, we conclude that they are of immense use to the US-Ireland Alliance in choosing our Mitchell Scholars, and we have recommended their use to other award programs. We will continue to strive to create an opportunity for candidates to best present themselves to us and tell us why they want to become Mitchell Scholars.

3

I Love It When a Grad Plan Comes Together
Graduate School Advising and the Truman Application

TARA YGLESIAS

Tara Yglesias has served as the deputy executive secretary of the Truman Foundation for the past five years and has been involved in the selection of Truman Scholars since 2001. During this time, she had the opportunity to study the trends and characteristics of each incoming class of scholars. She used this knowledge to assist in the development of new foundation programs and initiatives as well as the design of a new foundation website and online application system. An attorney by training, she began her career by spending six years in the Office of the Public Defender in Fulton County, Georgia. She specialized in trial work and serious felonies but also assisted with the training of new attorneys. A former Truman Scholar from Pennsylvania, she also served as a Senior Scholar at Truman Scholars Leadership Week and the foundation's Public Service Law Conference prior to joining the foundation's staff.

The Truman Scholarship staff spends a great deal of time trying to temper some of the unnecessary anxiety that surrounds the Truman application: The policy proposal, no matter how ridiculous, will cause problems only during the interview, and even then, it is unlikely to be fatal. The resource section, no matter whether a student decides on APA or MLA, will be given only a brief glance by a reader who is just trying to be sure the student looked at the right sources (and, quiet as it is kept, the reader may not even know the difference between APA and MLA). The Summer Institute question, no matter how forcefully the student answers "No!" will never derail an application. But of the remaining unloved and overlooked questions on the application, question 11[1]—where students describe their graduate programs—is the one that can play a critical role in both the success of the process on college campuses and the success of the application under review by the Truman selection committee.

This essay will cover graduate school advising for the Truman application, tips for advising, guidance on how the readers view this section of the application, and suggestions for the writing process. As ever, while some of these bits of wisdom may be applicable to a variety of applications, my expertise lies with the Truman Scholarship program. Advisors and students should apply these suggestions to other scholarships at their peril.

Advising: So Whaddaya Wanna Do with Your Life?

My extensive knowledge of how to advise students for graduate school comes from that one time I was a student who then applied for graduate school. As a first-generation college student, step one required someone to explain to me what graduate school was—I was a bit fuzzy on that point. But other than that confusion, I was every bit as obstinate and overconfident as I am today. Advising me was likely a nightmare. There was certainly a lot of skulking and eye rolling. But I did get advice—some good, some bad, all brief—which I then applied in haphazard ways to my Truman application. I wrote a tight, focused essay on attending law school with an emphasis on clinical experience.[2] But there were no soul-searching talks over International Coffee, no sudden realizations, and certainly no *feelings* of any kind. After my selection, when I was asked to speak with and mentor other Truman and Truman-like students, I could not figure out why so many wanted to talk so much about their hopes and dreams. I certainly could not imagine why someone would do such a thing with a professor, of all people. As it turned out, I was as much of a nightmare as an advisor as I was as an advisee. In short, there are professional graduate school advisors out there, perhaps reading this very sentence, who are eminently more qualified than I am to suggest how to advise students on graduate school selection.

But in my capacity at the Truman Foundation, I have vast and intensive experience cleaning up the mess made by unsuccessful graduate school advising.[3] Sometimes the problems in advising are evident in the application process. We see essays that are unformed or ill informed. We have interviews with students who seem unaware of the ramifications of their graduate school plans. But for scholars, these issues can spill over into their interaction with the foundation. We require graduate school proposals before we provide funding for scholars.[4] During this process, it becomes quite obvious who either did not receive or was not amenable to graduate school advising. But the profound difference here is that we will not cut a check to a student who is unable to provide a coherent graduate school plan.

But of all the fallout from unsuccessful graduate school advising, the worst may be the scholar with *graduate school regret.* We see them, ghostly shades wandering around our office moaning, "Why didn't anyone tell me law school is so boring?" "Everyone in my PhD program is petty and vengeful!" "No one at my [research UK masters program] even cares if I do the reading!" It can be gratifying to hear scholars say, "You told me not to do X, I did it. Now I'm miserable." But the chorus of despair does get to me after a while.

While a few of these students are the sort for whom no prior intervention would do any good, it does appear that some of these issues are preventable through the judicious dispensing of graduate school advice throughout the application process. The added benefit of providing this advice is that the graduate school portion of the Truman application process is the most portable of essays. No one may ever ask for two short sentences about the three most significant courses the student has taken, but the student can certainly reapply the information gathered in question 11 to future graduate school essays. Of all the feedback that we get from finalists, the majority of students mention how much the discussions about graduate school helped to clarify their goals.

To that end, here are a few suggestions about on-campus advising for graduate school:[5]

- *Talk early:* Whether the advising comes from the fellowships office or elsewhere on campus, early exposure to graduate school programs and the requirements thereof is critical to future Truman (and life) success. This advice is particularly true for first-generation students, who may not be aware of the need to preplan testing and course work to meet graduate school deadlines. Early advising will also help to get those students for whom graduate school is a vague and distant idea thinking about the Truman process. Students interested in advocacy—a prime breeding ground for Truman Scholars—often spend so much time in the early years of campus life chained to a fence in protest that they never even consider graduate school. We tend to run into these students much later in their careers—after they have worked for a while and now are working on the JD, MA, or PhD—and are left wondering whether they would have been outstanding Truman applicants if graduate school had appeared on the radar earlier.[6]

- *Talk often:* Students may enter an undergraduate program set on one idea (med school or bust) and cling to that idea no matter how their interests (policy wonkery is pretty cool) or abilities (Organic Chem: C-) evolve. Few young people have the ability to be self-reflective, so occasional "graduate school checkups" may be advisable. We see several applications a cycle where a student has had a clear pivot in direction; frequent advising check-ins could make this transition smoother both for the student and the application.

- *Talk only to the student:* One of the most difficult situations we face is when students' ideas are not their own. Pressures from family, professors, and even advisors can overshadow a student's own interests. This situation often comes wrapped in many complex emotional and cultural factors as well—making for a thorny problem when it comes to advising. Working with students so that they can express their own ideas and needs serves them best in the long run, but it is not always easy. One of the tricks that we use is to get students to visualize—really visualize—their lives at forty. Once we explain that forty will not come with Geritol and a hip replacement, scholars can understand the importance of being where they—and not their parents—want them to be. The conversation that the student needs to have with the interloper—be it a family or faculty member—may be difficult, but allowing students to express themselves authentically in their application is well worth the trouble.

- *Talk clearly:* Most students have some idea what they want to be when they grow up. The problem is that they have no idea how to get there. Starting with the dream job gives the student a concrete way to talk about what they want to do. From there, informational interviews can be a great way to get students to understand the next steps in the process and the graduate school options available to them.

- *Talk actual as well as intellectual:* Students often get caught up in the intellectual life of graduate school. While the rigor and content of programs are important, students should also have the opportunity to explore some of the more mundane issues of graduate education. Understanding the fundamental differences between the life of a graduate student and the life of an undergraduate student is important. We see many students who imagine graduate school is just one halcyon continuation of their undergraduate career. We all know this perception to be inaccurate—we should warn students that undergraduate hijinks are not appreciated in graduate school.

- *Talk to people other than professors:* There are people in the world who are useful and happy who do not have PhDs. For many students, however, PhDs are the only people from whom they seek graduate advice. Students should speak with at least two or three people who have, fairly recently, attended programs of interest to the student. For students at campuses with graduate schools, help arrange a time for them to talk to current graduate students interested in similar issues.

- *Talk in ways that are not overly proscriptive:* Sometimes, advising is just too easy: *I want revenge on those who wronged me!* Go to law school. *I want to learn more and more about less and less.* Consider a PhD. *I enjoy playing God and am good at organic chem.* Here's a med school brochure. But without pushing at these ideas, students will never be in a position to really explain why they want these degrees.

They will also not be able to defend these ideas against a harsh and unjust panel of dream crushers (the Truman interview panel) who want to do nothing more than throw every graduate school plan into the fire and dance around the embers (or so it sometimes seems to students who have not thought through their plans).[7]

- *A few things to remember:* The Truman is unique in that we allow students to take four years of deferral from the date that they complete their undergraduate education. In fact, we strongly encourage all students to take at least a year between undergraduate and graduate school. When advising students, be sure they are aware of this practice. For some, this information will reduce the pressure that they are feeling to figure out graduate school in this instant. Additionally, we do support study overseas if a student is interested in obtaining a degree from an international program.

Reading the Application: They Kill Dreams, Don't They?

Truman applications are evaluated on three main criteria: leadership, commitment to a career in public service, and likelihood of academic success in graduate school. Question 11 falls squarely within the third sphere, but its role in the application can have a direct impact on how we evaluate the other two.

Our Nominee Rating Form includes question 11 as part of the "Appropriateness for proposed graduate study program" category,[8] along with the student's transcript, questions 3, 6, 10, 11, 12, 13, Institution Nomination Letter, Continuing Academic Success Letter, and the policy proposal. This section considers "activities, grades, strength/depth and breadth of studies, quality of policy proposal, appropriateness of graduate study plans, likely appeal to institutions listed in Item 11." But while question 11 is one of many items considered in this category, both its location in the application and content make it an important tool for reviewers in evaluating an application.

The role of question 11 relates to the way our readers are taught to read applications.[9] Our applications are not simply read and ranked one against the other. We do not tally up public service commitments and leadership positions and select the applications with the most. We read the applications in search of change agents—and what a change agent looks like depends on an area of interest, individual circumstances, and even geographic location. That variation requires our readers to be flexible in their evaluation. A student who plans to have a global impact on a matter of public health will look very different from the student who plans to run for a leadership position in tribal government. The student wanting to emphasize the need for arts education will not share a lot of characteristics with the student who plans to create a fully realized neuron on a computer. We encourage our readers to recognize these differences. Rather than engaging in open combat to see which student has the most peer-reviewed articles published, readers just try to determine whether students have fully realized their potential to be change agents.

To do this type of evaluation, readers spend the bulk of the application review time information gathering. All through the nomination letter and questions 1 through 8 and question 10, readers are simply absorbing data. Question 9 is the first time a student has to present something other than a list of accomplishments. Question 9 is the amuse-bouche, in some ways: it *prepares* readers for what they are to see later in the application but can be satisfying in its own right. Extending the metaphor, question 11 then becomes a hearty appetizer for the main course of questions 12 and 13.[10]

Arriving at question 11, readers suddenly have a way to evaluate all the data they have been gathering. Does this student have the leadership, service commitment, and intellect necessary to succeed in this program? Has the student demonstrated a steadily increasing level of engagement? Does the student seem to have an understanding of how to make the changes that he or she seeks to make?

While question 11, on its face, provides information about graduate school, the subtext of this question is very important. Students need to demonstrate an understanding of how to tackle the problems they have identified. That understanding begins (and sometimes tragically ends) with an identification of what graduate school program will best prepare them for a career in public service.

The first threshold our readers look for is whether the graduate school plans "makes sense" for students and for issues. The sense-making threshold is often fairly low, but some students still fail to meet it. The most common issues are the following:

- *Graduate school plans that are unfocused:* Applicants still sometimes include responses that do not have degree programs listed. Others will give a general response about the importance of graduate school generally but fail to discuss any particulars.
- *Graduate school plans that are too inclusive:* Students sometimes propose unwieldy joint degrees that are essentially PhD/JD/MBAs. Whether this is hubris or uncertainty is unclear, but the response is problematic.
- *Graduate school plans that emerge from nowhere:* There should be some correlation between the student's activities, interests, and graduate program. If the response to question 11 is a surprise, the readers will not be pleased.

Once the threshold is met, readers then begin to evaluate the response in more detail. For the purposes of this essay, these steps appear to be discrete. In reality, this evaluation takes place quickly and in no particular order. We look to see whether students have identified the best degree program to work on their particular issue. This determination is, of course, a bit subjective. One reader may feel strongly that a policy degree is the best choice for a student, while another may think a PhD is more appropriate. But it is important that students make their decision process explicit in the essay so the readers can follow the rationale. "Showing their work" can also help if students are selected for interview, as it will reassure panelists that selected finalists did not arrive at their degree programs lightly.

From there, the readers will look to see if the student identified the best institution for the selected degree. This determination can take into account institution specialties, the student's strengths, and institutional prestige. Readers look for specific information about institutional offerings to see whether the student has reviewed the program thoroughly. We use these distinctions to set programs apart. The readers look to see whether the student has the appropriate course work and interests for individual institutions. Institutional prestige can also be an important factor. Our readers do not make direct comparisons on degree programs, so a student who proposes the number 1 urban planning degree in the country will not be given a higher score than the student who proposes the number 653 urban planning degree in the country. But students whose career paths are dependent on attending a prestigious program had best select graduate institutions accordingly. Conversely, our readers recognize also that some students have criteria other than prestige (family commitments, geographical, or financial constraints) at play when selecting a graduate school.

A full one-third of our reading panels are graduate school admissions personnel or individuals who have been involved with the accreditation process for specific types of graduate schools. The remaining members of the reading panel are Truman Scholars who have attended the graduate school programs most sought after by Truman applicants. Their level of knowledge is extensive and detailed. They are quickly able to discern which students have done their homework and which have not.

The final factor is to determine whether the stated degree and program make sense for the student. While an applicant may have identified the premier doctoral program for international relations and deftly explained why such a credential would allow work on issues of human trafficking in Asia, the applicant must still make the case that the degree is appropriate. Readers look to the data they have gathered from the rest of the application to determine whether the student's abilities are likely to be a good fit for the program.

But that is not to say that we have never selected applicants with poor question 11 responses. Our readers and panelists all know that we will provide graduate school advising as part of the Truman process. If an applicant has a poor answer to question 11 but otherwise possesses the qualities of a Truman Scholar, the readers or panelists will forgive the applicant. But a failure in question 11 means that other parts of the application will need to work much harder to overcome the deficit. In an interview, a poor question 11 can mean the student spends precious interview time defending a decision to go or not to go to law school.

Writing the Application: Advice for Advisors and Students

Much ink has been spilled over the issue of advisors and their role in the editing process. The Truman Foundation thinks it is not appropriate for advisors to do hard edits on applications. But asking questions, providing feedback, and offering students ways to improve their writing are all appropriate. For our application, question 11 is probably the place where advisor feedback is most welcomed and expected. Advisors do not know more about their students' leadership experiences than they do, but advisors almost certainly know more about graduate school. In most cases, advisors have attended/worked at/parked near/taught in a graduate school for more years than the students have been alive. It is absolutely appropriate to give feedback on these essays both in terms of content (directing students to investigate other programs and degrees where appropriate) and style (assisting students with expressing these ideas more effectively). If a student writes, "I plan to get a PhD in anthropology because such a credential will ensure that I receive respect and deference from my colleagues," then once the advisor has stopped laughing and wiped away the tears, it is appropriate to discuss where the student obtained the information and how this information might be perceived in an interview context (hint: also with laughter).

In terms of content, the most common mistakes are these:

- Overcredentialing: *"After obtaining my JD and PhD, I will begin my career as a program analyst at the Department of Justice."* Students seem to believe that the way to prove to us that they are smart is by obtaining a complete assortment of letters after their name. There are very, very few people for whom such an ambitious graduate school plan makes sense. Presenting the Whitman's Sampler of graduate degrees only serves to make the student look ill informed. If the multidegree trajectory is born of indecision rather than over-ambition, the student is better served by just being honest about the indecision.
- Undercredentialing: *"Once I get my MD from Hollywood Upstairs Medical School, I plan to begin my career with Médecins Sans Frontières."* This phenomenon occurs less often, but it is still common enough to be a concern. Students need to demonstrate that they understand the reality of their situation. If a top-tier graduate program is not within their reach, their career goals should match their future credentials. If the student plans a career within international organizations, the student should select a top-tier program that will have international cachet.
- Puffery: *"Third-Tier University is simply the best place to get an MPA."* We see this most often when students want to attend a school for

reasons other than academic reputation. Perhaps they want to stay local to continue political involvement, to be near family, or for financial reasons. Readers would much rather an explicit statement of intent than an attempt to convince them that every ranking available of MPA programs is wrong.

- Graduate admissions materials presented as fact: *"MBA degrees present the single best outside-the-box way to have impactful, dynamic change in the synergistic paradigm of the public sector."* Students must be critical consumers of graduate school information. Parroting back slogans from graduate school brochures is a sure way to have a reader scrawl "naive" all over the comment sheet. For obvious reasons, students who propose MBA programs tend to fall for this trick most often. Our preference against MBA programs has been stated before,[11] but should advisors have the rare student for whom the MBA makes sense, they should encourage that student not to play Business Buzzword Bingo with the application.

- Omission: *"I plan to go directly to law school. I have no latent desire to study in the United Kingdom even if someone else is paying."* Students who plan to apply to a UK scholarship program or take time to work before graduate school or get a Fulbright to Argentina should put that in question 11. There is no reason why any of these plans would make us less likely to award the Truman; in most cases we would be more likely to award it. If students have other constraints on their graduate school plans—military service, financial considerations, family obligations—these should be included in question 11.

- Imprecise language: *"A JD is the best degree to prepare me for my career in education policy."* This issue arises most often with those students who want to get professional degrees but do not want to ever act as members of that profession. The bulk of the student's application focuses on policy concerns, but question 11 still contains a trip to law or medical school. It is often difficult to determine whether this problem is one of degree selection—perhaps the student does not quite understand the value of a policy degree—or one of sloppy writing. Students who submit applications with this issue should prepare for the eventuality of being interrogated on the difference between a policy degree and a professional degree.

- Wasted space: *"While in law school, I plan to take the first year, or 1L, curriculum which includes . . ."* Our reading committee is comprised of a variety of people from a variety of backgrounds. Several of them are graduate school admissions officers or deans. A few even attended the program that the student is writing about. There is no reason to approach an essay about Harvard Law School as if we are wholly unfamiliar with Harvard or the study of law. This issue is the most frustrating. We often never hear the student's motivations because we are too busy reading through a listing of core course work.

- Dense space: *"A Masters in Embedded Systems from the KTH Royal Institute of Technology would, of course, be the best choice for me."* The inverse of wasted space finds us with degree programs that are wholly unfamiliar. These programs are often highly technical and specialized, which often means that students come from insulated programs and do not always know that regular people have no idea what computational neurobiology is. Help students to identify which programs are less well known and suggest ways to explain these programs for a lay audience.

- Failure to show work: *"I will attend medical school in Sweden."* For most students, writing a response to question 11 requires a lot of thinking and research. Yet so many students do not feel compelled to share that information with us. If the program the student identified begs a question like "Why not an MPH?" Or "do you even speak Swedish?", the student can save readers some confusion and save the interview panelists some time by including that information.

- Failure to persuade: *"My choice of law school has the highest judicial clerkship placement in the country."* This is the inverse to "failure to show work." In an effort to demonstrate all the research they have done, as well as a reflection of the odd things that one can find on the Internet, students are beginning to incorporate some truly unpersuasive factoids into these essays. Thus far in 2015, I have seen this example sentence in three separate essays—none of them were for the same school. Such bits of ridiculata serve only to pad the essay and provide little context.

- Failure to address deficiencies: *"Pay no attention to the lack of quantitative course work behind the curtain."* Our readers are well aware of the general qualifications required to get into these graduate school programs. An applicant missing some crucial component should address this item briefly in question 11. A simple acknowledgment that the student needs to take additional course work or will have to overcome a lack of professional experience will only serve to enhance the essay and demonstrate that the student has done appropriate research.

- Failure to address uncertainty: *"Even though I haven't taken a single course in economics, the PhD in Applied Economics is for me!"* Believe it or not, it is perfectly acceptable for a student to express some uncertainty in the application. A student who is willing to grapple with these issues, rather than blindly charging into the fray, can be a compelling candidate.

Once the student's application is in perfect shape, then advisors need only to determine the best way to memorialize all of that hard work. In general, we do not need a lot of information about the degree program in the letter of nomination. But the nomination letter might be the better place to address deficiencies in detail. If advisors know that a student lacks strong economics course work but plans to take it next semester, they can introduce that idea early to reassure the readers that these issues are being resolved. The nomination letter is also a good place to discuss the research the student did to select the degree—particularly if the student lacks room to do so coherently. Finally, be certain that the degree that is described in the Faculty Nomination letter is the same as the one proposed by the student. If a student proposes an MPP, the letter should mirror that language.[12]

Conclusion: Our Little Secret

After all this work—the gnashing of teeth and rending of garments, the soul-searching talks and extensive research, the informational interviews and coaching—it turns out that we do not really care if the student ever gets the degree proposed.

In fact, we spend much of our early relationship with students trying to get them to think about other degree paths and programs. We cajole them into taking years off. We hector them about switching degrees, dropping the joint program, or adding another degree. We undo all of the advisor's precious work.

But in the end, the scholars and our program are better for it. Graduate school advising is a moving target. But by encouraging critical thinking about graduate school from the beginning of the application process, advisors are ensuring the next generation of public service leaders is prepared for the challenges ahead, even if one of the first challenges is trying to get the Truman review committee to agree to their joint degree programs.

Notes

1. The text of question 11: *Describe the graduate education program you plan to pursue if you receive a Truman Scholarship.*

2. I reviewed my application for this article. The essay was officially *not bad*. It was dry and generic but overall fine.

3. Word choice is a struggle here. Sometimes, the advising is ineffective— the faculty advisor does not provide appropriate feedback and advice. Other times, the student is the problem and either will not or cannot process good advice when given. *Unsuccessful* seemed to capture both of these circumstances.

4. These proposals are extensive. We require a narrative that covers how this graduate school program fits into the scholar's career objectives, complete curriculum for the program including professors with whom the scholar plans to work, a plan for internships and summer work, a comparison of this program with other similar programs, as well as information about how many graduates from the school go into public service upon graduation. More details are found here: http://www.truman.gov/graduate-school-proposal.

5. All suggestions are entirely doable in your copious free time.

6. Also remember that scholars can defer their scholarship for at least four years after they graduate college. So students who are certain they want to work for several years—or who are not even certain when they will attend graduate school—are still eligible.

7. Truman selection panels are not really like this description. But if the perception helps to motivate students to do a little introspection, so be it.

8. A copy of the form can be found here: http://www.truman.gov/nominee -rating-form.

9. The term *reader* refers to the members of our Finalist Selection Committee. This committee makes the initial cut of applications and determines who will be named a finalist. Once students are named finalists, they are interviewed by the members of our Regional Review Panels—referred to as "panelists."

10. Which sets up question 14 to be dessert. This arrangement sounds about right as 14 is sometimes perfect and other times entirely too much.

11. For us, the jury is still out on whether these degrees prepare students for careers in public service. It is a rare student for whom the MBA—as opposed to a PhD, MA, MPA/MPP, MUP, or any other public service–oriented degree— would be the best option. Additionally, the track record of scholars who attend business school is mixed at best.

12. While we are on this subject, MPP versus MPA is not a debate worth having. The difference in program seems to have more to do with when the program was established and the research of current faculty members than anything else. Please see Yongbeom Hur and Merl Hackbart, "MPA vs. MPP: A Distinction without a Difference?" *Journal of Public Affairs Education* 15, no. 4: 397–424; http://www.naspaa.org/jpaemessenger/article/v15n4-hur.pdf.

Part II

Advisors on the Process

4

The Personal Statement

JENNI QUILTER

Jenni Quilter is the director of the Office of National Scholarships at New York University (NYU), where she is also an assistant clinical professor in the Expository Writing Program. She has taught at NYU for seven years, though this is her first year in fellowships advising. She has also taught at Oxford University, where she completed her MPhil and DPhil in English Literature as a Rhodes Scholar from New Zealand. She writes mostly about visual art, but other essays have been published in Poetry, Agni, Southwest Review, *and* Nowhere. *Her most recent book is* New York School Painters and Poets: Neon in Daylight *(2014).*

The personal statement tends to induce a kind of vertigo in students. We may be used to sketching our lives in conversation, but it is another matter entirely to put pen to paper. Beyond wedding vows or eulogies, I cannot think of another occasion in our lives in which we are asked to make sense of how our private and public selves connect. It is hard to know which thought is more terrifying: what a life looks like compressed into a thousand words, or the fact that a life can be compressed this way. It is not surprising that applicants suffer the terror of the definitive, the way in which years need to be summed up in a sentence or two. What feels uncontainable needs to be contained. What seems completely self-evident has to be reflected upon.

The personal statement for the Rhodes Scholarship, in which applicants explain why they want to attend Oxford and what they plan to study, has always been a crucial part of the application. There are no other essays to write, no extensive short-answer or long-answer application questions, no other opportunity in which to directly explain why. Applicants have a chance to speak for themselves, to not let their achievements do the talking. In addressing the committee, the applicants can develop a cadence and rhythm in their sentences, exposing, in a new way altogether, the depth of the application.

Early this year, the Rhodes Trust at Oxford University issued a new directive about the personal statement, which has clear implications for the ways future applicants will approach the writing process. The Trust announced that from that point on, all applicants would be required to sign the following statement:

> *I attest that this personal statement is my own work and is wholly truthful. Neither it nor any earlier draft has been edited by anyone other than me, nor has anyone else reviewed it to provide me with suggestions to improve it. I understand that any such editing or review would disqualify my application.*

The wording is unequivocal. This means not just an injunction on textual review by fellowships advisors but also on verbal comment by professors, mentors, friends, or family.

In 2000, I wrote my personal statement for the Rhodes in my apartment in Auckland, New Zealand. I was twenty years old. I remember working myself up into tears on at least one occasion, telling my boyfriend then that I could not finish the application; it was just too stressful. I remember him hugging me. I am certain he read it in order to comfort me further. I know I also showed an early draft to Elizabeth Wilson, one of my professors, because I remember her sighing and looking up at me.

"What is it that you really want to do?" she asked.

"I want to write," I said, "but there are mitigating factors to that." It seemed impossible to make a living from writing in New Zealand.

"Put that," she said.

Under the Trust's guidelines, Ms. Wilson's review of my essay and her clarifying comment (which had editorial direction) are no longer allowed. My boyfriend would not have been able to look at a draft either.

There were no fellowships advisors at The University of Auckland.[1] The careers office told me that if I wanted to study English literature overseas at a graduate level, there were only two scholarships I could apply for: one to Oxford, and the other to Cambridge (the Prince of Wales scholarship). No one told me I could apply directly to colleges in the United States. In other words, I was a world away from where I found myself six months ago, mid-2014, at a conference for new fellowships advisors, organized by NAFA in Des Moines, Iowa. I had recently taken up the position of director of the Office of National Scholarships at New York University, where I had taught essay writing for the past seven years. In that time, I had acclimated to living in New York and teaching within a liberal arts degree program, but I had never stopped to imagine the industry involved in advising on scholarships, or its potential for professionalization. I should have, but I did not. So in Des Moines, I felt like a greenhorn. I had not been appointed for any administrative skill, and though it had not been said out loud, the reasoning was probably that if I had won a Rhodes, I could help others do it too.

This assumption worried me for all kinds of reasons, not in the least that when I first arrived in Oxford, it seemed that there were two kinds of Rhodes Scholars: Americans and everyone else. Each group had a different sense of how to mark and frame achievement. To speculate in more detail would possibly reveal more about my own insecurities at the time than anything else, but I do not think many Rhodes Scholars (at least from my time) would disagree that there was a difference between what the Americans had to do or be or want to win a Rhodes, and what the other scholars from other countries expected for themselves. Sitting in Des Moines, I was certain that had I grown up in the United States, I would not have won a Rhodes. I had been hired for expertise I did not have.[2]

The Rhodes Trust directive was referred to more than once at the NAFA conference. I can see why. It would be hard not to feel implicated by the Trust's reasoning:

> *The reason for the requirement is simple. We have concluded that, in many cases, the personal statements have become highly edited and formulaic productions that do not accurately reflect the applicant's actual writing style, personal story, or educational objectives. Fundamentally, they are no longer the work of the applicant.*

Who would develop this formula, if not fellowships advisors at universities?

The irony, at least to me, was that very few (if any) in the room were aware of such a formula. We were all beginning our jobs and struggling to get a handle on the basic calendar of deadlines and the differences between each scholarship. Many were taking up this role at their college in addition to their other teaching and/or administrative commitments, and so the focus was often on juggling responsibilities and developing good working relationships with the registrar's office and faculty. In other words, we were anything but slick. I think we would have all been horrified by the suggestion that we would ever tell a student what to write. We simply would not know what to advise.

Yet that is not quite right either. When I first heard about the Rhodes Trust's directive, before I had taken this job or even knew that NAFA existed, I still felt a hot rush of guilt. I felt implicated as a teacher; the Trust's criticism touched a nerve in me about the relationship between teaching and influence.

When I was an undergraduate, watching my professors reason out loud was a crucial turning point in my life. Before then, I knew you could have a writing style, but I had never realized you could have a thinking style. I fell in love with each approach; in, for instance, Ms. Wilson's dry, elliptical references to Elizabeth Bishop's biography, her silence at a student's ill-advised comment, her dogged persistence in thinking about one line, one word: *that* word in *that* line. Here were voices that were intimate without being confessional; they had character in the old-fashioned sense. Learning to master another's discourse is part and parcel of a university experience, and as with any language learning, mimicry is a fundamental part of the process. Though I would not have put it that way then, I developed my own voice only because I subsumed myself in others'. This involves a kind of self-abnegation, and it was a crucial step in developing my sense of intellectual integrity. It seems paradoxical to put the self in abeyance in order to strengthen it, but I would go so far as to say that it is a crucial part of the educational process.

Who I am as a teacher today is partly because of Ms. Wilson. I would never give up that experience—and yet I am also worried about influencing my own students the same way. Instinctively, I do not want to make too much of a mark (or if I do, I want it to be easily misidentified). I am wary of charismatic teaching and the sense of ego it implies. The basic tenet in offering an education (that they are there to learn and that you will guide them) ends up looking like a formula, particularly if what you teach starts to ossify with time and repetition. If you can rattle it off the top of your head, then they will be able to as well. It is very easy to slip from encouraging students to think about how they write, to telling them what to write. Asking students to listen and learn but then to also develop their own response is fraught with small but significant moments of ethical complication.

In the rush of the semester and in large classes, it is very easy to overlook or push past these awkward negotiations. Besides, students often present themselves as having learned a subject before they can even identify its complications. They learn quickly to ventriloquize a sense of certainty, and what mastery they do attain is often formulaic, partly because they are used to thinking instrumentally, to working out the shortest route between a task and its completion. This study tactic stands them in good stead with a busy schedule, but this sense of instrumental urgency can result in blithe academic jargon. The disparity between how students sound in class, casually chatting, and how they sound on paper is often so sizable that their best option (it seems) is to ignore it. Professors also easily overlook this disparity, chalking it up to a distinction between professional and private discourse. But the difference can also translate to a disingenuousness. If the Trust's observation about "highly edited and formulaic productions" could easily be applied to term papers in general, it seems worthwhile asking about the roots of this drive toward a glib mastery.

Two years ago, I spent one summer teaching a course in critical writing and thinking to high school students in the United Arab Emirates. One of the course objectives was to prepare them for university, and I taught a unit on writing the personal statement for college admission. Many of them were applying to colleges in the United States, and so I decided to prepare myself by buying an anthology of successful college application essays.

I was completely horrified. I still remember telling my colleague who was co-teaching the course, "But . . . but these are terrible!" She gave me a look that suggested cultural differences were afoot. Nonetheless even now, seven years into living in the United States, these essays still seem cutesy, overly general, and far too smug. Recollections of personal tragedy and difficulty are milked far too enthusiastically for my liking. They end with homilies that are so broad that no one could disagree, but few would want to discuss. That these are formulas is implicitly obvious, even if this sounds oxymoronic. You just have to read between the lines.

Let's say you wanted to show you were a mature, altruistic, worldly individual who believed in the power of education and giving back. Begin your arresting narrative with a number of concrete visual details. Your reader will be right next to you as you peer through the grimy windshield of the car rattling its way to an economically disadvantaged and/or socially disenfranchised community. Describe the pseudonymous child you taught how to read, respectfully noting that it was not the teacher's fault but the result of a far broader crisis of resources. Give a few affecting details about the classroom: the child's face, the way the light came in through the windows. Acknowledge it was difficult, but that you persevered. Quietly insist that this afternoon is evidence of your general lifelong commitment to learning. The possibility that this moment was genuinely meaningful (remember, for both you and the child) is entirely masked by the stylistic formula you have employed to describe the event. The epiphany is ready-to-wear. If this is the intellectual sense of self that students present and use to gain admission to universities, then the ethical implications are clear. If this formula is not challenged in college, they will continue to go on using it.

I could be making too much of this, but consider, for a moment, how draconian the Rhodes Trust directive seems to be. It flies in the face of best practice in writing, namely, that we test our words out on a reader prior to publication, whether it be an editor, fellow writer, or significant other. We need the physical fact of another person, a consciousness different from ours. I did precisely that with five people with this essay. Watching someone else read our own words, we suddenly see how our sentences appear to another. It is almost as physical as a film dissolve; the words themselves appear changed, as if the reader picked them up and set them down, a fraction of an inch to the left or the right. One sentence seems suddenly disconnected from the next. Another is obviously a place-holder for a far more interesting thought. In drafts, we do not see how we can be direct because we are afraid of appearing overly simple, yet we also shy away from thoughts we have not clarified in our minds yet. We need a reader to call us out, to tell us when we are not making sense, even when we desperately want to.

The members of the Trust likely know this, which suggests that the problem they are addressing is so formidable that they will consider putting one basic tenet of writing aside to preserve another even more fundamental. Presumably, the students turning up for interview did not match who they were on paper. Their personal statements lacked a sense of ethos—by which I mean the sense that value and character are intimately tied to voice and that these things are mutually sustaining. If students do not have a voice of their own, then they cannot act with integrity (the state of being whole and undivided) in a wide variety of contexts. The Rhodes Trust would rather have an underdeveloped sense of self than no real sense at all. Ethos can be taught, or at least, students can be encouraged to develop their own ethos. But it is a complicated negotiation, and one that verges on being a contradiction in terms.

Fourteen years ago when I sat down to write the personal statement, in my naïveté I took the task literally. I thought they wanted a snapshot of who I was at the time, a compression of what was important to me, the basic physical routines of my life, and also the ideas I was thinking about. I began with my living circumstances (a flat, a best friend, a boyfriend, a cat called Luca) and discussed some of my writing projects. This might sound like a terrible voice-over from the opening credits of a sitcom, but I had not watched shows like *Felicity* and had not internalized the cognitive dissonance involved in that kind of self-reflection, namely, that I might be struggling, but other people would aspire to be me. The word *aspirational* is treated very differently in New Zealand than it is in the United States. I was not living anyone else's dream, even unconsciously, so I think my writing had the flatness of fact. I tried to convey the horizontal sprawl of days, what my life actually felt like. It was torturous to compress my daily existence down in this way, to miniaturize what already seemed so puny, but the size of the essay forced me to make connections between things that would have been otherwise lost, between my interest in Maori politics and self-determination, and my ideas about modernist poetry, along with the poetry I was writing. The exact combination of these topics was so particular that I must have come across as a very odd fish indeed. But in writing the statement, I was confronted by patterns that would have otherwise dawned slowly, if at all. I do not have a copy of the essay, and I cannot remember exactly what I wrote, but I do remember really struggling to make sense of these topics' relatedness. Each subject was a symptom, and I was trying to diagnose the illness.

I can imagine that had I gone to a fellowships advisor, I would have written a very different personal statement. I might have thought more about my life vertically, as a series of hills and summits I had mastered, and recalled stories that showed rather than told my promise as an academic or a leader. It would have been a functional essay and a clear indication of my priorities and ambition, but it would also have been shaped quite distinctly by what the Rhodes Trust said they were looking for, and the experience of reading it would have been like watching someone waltzing by herself, hands reaching into thin air. My naive, idiosyncratic interpretation of the prompt would have disappeared. The new essay would have been personal but not as private.

Because we often do not know our students' lives well, we ask them to represent themselves in parts; it is easier to digest. But this delays the work of the whole, the deep fascia of connection that is a mark of ethos. I could imagine obediently accepting a fellowships advisor's copyediting and revisions, the suggestions of other words or key terms, without thinking twice about it. My advisor had done this before. She was an adult. Other people had won scholarships; I had not. In the face of such overwhelming odds, I think I would have willingly abdicated my integrity because I would not have seen it as an abdication but rather as a translation, as if I were simply communicating my point in a language other than my own. And if she had provided feedback on my draft once, twice, even nineteen times, I would have been immersed in her ethos as fully as I was in any of my other classes.

Signs of students' basic obedience flash by so quickly we barely notice them. A personal statement formula does not have to be consciously understood for it to be a formula; we can sense it and choose to rush past it without naming the pattern, as we might the broader themes of a novel. Part of the pleasure in reading is that sense of emergent knowledge (in coming to know rather than being told), and it feels particularly blissful when it seems effortless; we know even if we do not quite know how. If we are enjoying ourselves, we often delay creating what feels like a crude rendering of an idea or text. But that delay does not stop a pattern of meaning from quietly thriving. The manipulation the Trust is pointing toward is not necessarily Machiavellian. We do not have to consciously manipulate our students; we can stand by quite innocently, watching them write, those complicated patterns of authority and obedience and the desire to please already firmly embedded in the student-teacher relationship, knowing that they will do the instinctive math on their own, especially if we give them sample essays to read.

What, then, can or should we do? For one, we can make students more aware of the complexity of the problem. We all behave and write disingenuously at times, and some of our mistakes are honest ones. My recollection of writing the Rhodes personal statement at the beginning of this essay was framed (as one of my readers put it in an email) "in a very personal statement-y way." It is so easy to overestimate the emotional latency of basic details in our own lives. My readers have no idea what living in my apartment in Auckland in 2000 was actually like; that sentence triggers nothing in them, and everything in me. The brevity of a personal statement means that I cannot give them much more. What I am writing has the portentousness of a haiku, but it is really, really easy to write bad haiku when trying to be meaningful. Students often complain about the conundrum of length and depth when they are writing their personal statements, and I cheerfully brush it off, but I am starting to think that it is a serious constraint that needs to be approached more mindfully, in the same fashion that screenwriters talk about "inciting incidents," or novelists the issue of "voice." My students would be better equipped if they understood brevity as a challenge of the genre with aesthetic implications (how *does* one convey psychological depth?) rather than as a stupid word limit.

Secondly, students are not always encouraged to notice or write about how they might consciously or unconsciously absorb and take up the intellectual ideas they encounter in their classes. There is a good reason for this; the first signs of relatedness often feel narcissistic (e.g., "Marx's theory of alienation reminds me of the time I had a paper route . . ."). As first-year students, they are encouraged to get themselves out of the way in order to really focus on the theory at hand, and so the writing style they develop for term papers tends to keep these ideas at arms' length. But a personal statement often indirectly asks for the opposite. We are fascinated by well-written displays of fascination. We want to know what broader patterns of thinking motivate a life, and to turn an analytical eye on these patterns is to show an instinct for critical thinking. But to reverse the critical gaze this way, to turn it away from another text and onto the writer's own life, requires a flexibility that comes from time and practice.

It could be rather drily noted that this recalibration is surely the point of a liberal arts degree; what I am describing is not the work of a fellowships advisor so much as that of the university in general. But this means that the personal statement is the canary in the coal mine; it tells us whether the institution has succeeded in following through on its lofty aims. And because this kind of sustained intellectual development involves repetition, fellowships advising should be focused not just on short-term, draft-specific projects but on developing exercises and techniques, teaching scales and arpeggios, rather than perfecting one piece alone.

This means shifting the distribution of teaching labor within a scholarship calendar cycle. A significant portion of my teaching/advising has to be done before they sit down to write the personal statement.

There is precedent for this. At the conference in Des Moines, one panel devoted to the personal statement covered the basics: a personal statement is not a résumé, journal, academic article, or plea for special dispensation, but a story, an invitation for the reader to get to know you, an indication of your priorities and judgment. These are the structuring phrases of Mary Tolar's excellent "Definition of a Personal Statement," a go-to text that was recommended to me by numerous people in a variety of contexts. Tolar herself was an American Rhodes Scholar and a central figure in the founding of NAFA.

What is striking is that Tolar's guidance has everything to do with how students conceptualize their approach to the task: how they begin rather than end. And this emphasis is quite different from the Trust's sense of a controlling voice, that ghost in the machine that the Trust must have begun to sense in the personal statements they were receiving. It is clear, though, that the central issue is not that other voices will show up in a student's writing, but how they integrate them. Had I worked with a fellowships advisor on my personal statement, I would have eventually learned to absorb her voice rather than be absorbed by it, but I am reasonably certain that this growth would have occurred over a time frame longer than one or two months. This process might have sped up if I had been made aware of this absorptive process and consciously experimented in how these voices might well be multiple. T. S. Eliot famously observed that "immature poets imitate; mature poets steal." Students need to know the difference between imitating and stealing, to have a robust enough sense of self, however instinctive, that is conscious enough to know the difference. My advising ought to be focused on cultivating this consciousness in students.

The benefit of a regular writing class is that it teaches students through repetition to internalize the voices of readers around them, to do more of that reseeing, that revisioning work on their own before turning to ask another to read. I need to create this collective effect, even when I am working one-on-one. As a fellowships advisor, I am not helping the students to translate anything at all. I am not "explaining" or "putting" something in a "better way." They need to have confidence in their own drafting instincts.

One way to encourage this confidence is to point out to students that they have more models than they think they have. The essay is enjoying a revival right now, and writers like Leslie Jamison, David Foster Wallace, and John Jeremiah Sullivan are widely read. Of course, they have the luxury of the long form, and the compression required for a thousand-word statement is something else altogether. But there are great anthologies of short nonfiction, like *In Short* (edited by Judith Kitchen and Mary Paumier Jones), that would widen the range of a student's imagination and ambition so much more effectively than those published collections of personal statements for college applications, which are unreadable beyond their immediate audience and objective. No one would buy one of those books "just to read." To me, this is a sign of bad writing.

I am aware this is a highly subjective assertion; so let me suggest, less baldly, that a text's significance cannot be completely contextual; there should be, at the very least, an attempt to make visible the larger significance of an idea to an unknown reader. The possibility of communication with someone we do not know is one of the most fundamental and thrilling promises of writing. A student ought to lean in to this demand rather than avoiding that responsibility by assuming the personal statement is a highly instrumental set of cabalistic signs that simply need to be put in the right order for a very particular reader. It is true that when writing a personal statement for a scholarship, an applicant's sense of a reader is more complicated than a novelist's or nonfiction writer's. Students know they are writing, somewhat paradoxically, for both an undetermined and limited set of readers. But even naming this paradox as a distinctive feature of the genre might help students think more mindfully about what it is they are doing. Cultivating this self-awareness might help them to write a personal statement on their own—be capable, even, of managing the substantial handicap of having no prior reader at all.

Notes

1. It could be argued that Ms. Wilson acted as a fellowships advisor; it just was not "official." After all, professors frequently offer advice about scholarships based on their experience and inclination, and the degree to which fellowships advising is formalized as part of either a faculty or administrative job varies greatly. Nonetheless, I think there is a distinct difference between what Ms. Wilson did and what I do now. Students from all over the university can contact me because my role has been formally named. I only had Ms. Wilson's advice because I was her student.

2. The notion that the American Rhodes competition is selecting a different kind of Rhodes Scholar than Commonwealth countries is a contentious one, and really deserves a much more careful explanation. I have thought long and hard about including such a bold, unsubstantiated, and vague claim (it is the kind that would get my own students in trouble), but I know to not acknowledge this difference would be to elide a central caveat with my argument here; namely, that I feel qualified to weigh into this debate about the personal statement as a teacher of writing, not as a Rhodes Scholar.

5

Exploring One's Life for Others
Reflections on Writing the Personal Statement

LOWELL T. FRYE

Lowell T. Frye is the Elliott Professor of Rhetoric and Humanities at Hampden-Sydney College, in Virginia, where since 2008 he has also been the director of the Office of Fellowship Advising. A teacher of writing and literature, he has written on the novels of Walter Scott; the ghost stories of Amelia Edwards, M. E. Braddon, and E. Nesbit; and (with his spouse Elizabeth J. Deis) British views of America in the 1830s. His primary scholarly engagement, however, has been with the work of Thomas Carlyle, nineteenth-century British historian and man of letters. In 2012 he delivered the Thomas Green Lecture to the Carlyle Society at the University of Edinburgh, on "'Leaving Hugh Blair's Lectures Quite Behind': Thomas Carlyle's Rhetorical Revolution." He earned his BA in English from Saint John's University in Minnesota, and his MA and PhD in English from Duke University.

First, a disclaimer: what follows is not, or at least not primarily, detailed practical advice about how to write the personal statement that is a required part of many national scholarship competitions. Others before me have offered excellent advice for those in search of it: Anthony Cashman, fellowships director at the College of the Holy Cross, provides lucid, practical guidance about what a personal statement is—and is not—and describes succinctly what he calls "the three fundamental moves of personal statements and applications."[1] Joe Schall has earned the gratitude of fellowships advisors and scholarship applicants alike for the writing advice available on his website Writing Personal Statements Online.[2] And as a fellowships advisor for the past seven years, I am as aware as my colleagues at other institutions that valuable advice on writing personal statements is to be found on the websites of fellowship offices at colleges and universities across the country.

The very volume of advice on writing the personal statement paradoxically suggests both that there is a large audience for such guidance and that no amount of practical advice about *what* a personal statement is and *how* to write one ever suffices. Rather than adding to the stock of excellent tactical guidance, therefore, I will instead draw on my experience as a teacher of rhetoric to suggest why the task of writing an effective personal statement is so difficult—and yet potentially so rewarding—for most undergraduates, whether or not the scholarship application is successful.

Writing an engaging personal statement for a scholarship competition is a complex rhetorical task that requires probing self-reflection and an acute awareness of audience, to say nothing of stylistic fluency. Self-reflection on its own is insufficient, for it is the dynamic rhetorical interplay among the specific writer, the specific audience, and the specific scholarship occasion that generates vivid and meaningful personal statements.

Let me begin by situating what I wish to say about writing the personal statement by thinking for a moment about the particular students I work with at Hampden-Sydney College, a small, selective, independent liberal arts college for men in south-central Virginia. Most Hampden-Sydney students are of traditional college age. Like their peers at other colleges, many Hampden-Sydney students have more academic potential than they initially realize. The students I work with in my capacity as fellowships advisor usually rank in the top 10 percent of their college class, and many of them eventually earn election to the campus chapter of Phi Beta Kappa. But still they are young men between the ages of eighteen and twenty-two, somewhere between boyhood and manhood, not yet fully formed, and so it is no surprise that they encounter difficulty in crafting a personal statement that requires a keen sense of self. I hesitate to generalize too broadly from my experiences at Hampden-Sydney (it is, after all, one of only four men's colleges remaining in the United States) to make claims about students at colleges or universities with a different mission or demographic. Still, my observations about the personal statement—and the students who write them—may have value that extends beyond the local.

The Students

One of the mottoes of Hampden-Sydney College is inscribed in Latin on its front gates: *Huc venite iuvenes ut exeatis viri.* Enter here as youths so that you may leave as men. Note the assumption here: no matter where they enroll, traditional college students come to us as works in progress, no longer boys or girls but not yet men or women. No matter how gifted they are intellectually when they arrive, they have much more to learn. No matter how accomplished they are when they arrive, they are still in many ways neophytes. Even the best of our students—and all of us, as fellowships advisors, work with many of the strongest students in our respective institutions—are outwardly confident but inwardly doubtful about their abilities and place in the world. They are ambitious in a general, unformulated way; they want to make a difference in the world, they want to be "successful," broadly defined, but they often lack clear goals or an identified path toward those goals. They are very much living in the present, and to the extent that they are thinking about the future (as opposed to feeling a diffused anxiety about employment after graduation), they are still not clear about what they want to do or why. They are, in other words, just like most of us were at a comparable age.

Even the few who seek out a fellowships advisor because they have begun to think about applying for a scholarship most often do not have a clear understanding of themselves, let alone the demands and requirements of the scholarship opportunity or how that particular scholarship meshes with their ambitions. Students at Hampden-Sydney—and I wager students at most American colleges and universities—tend to be uncertain and even evasive if asked pointed questions about their goals, their desires, their plans. And because their doubt is troubling, even to them, they tend to mask their uncertainty either with an ironic detachment from commitment or with a bustle of activities that keep them busy and therefore insulated from the difficult task of thinking about the future. It is easy to get students to provide surface details about what they are doing, but it is much harder to get them to talk seriously about their beliefs, their worries, their hopes. I know this from personal experience as a teacher of college writing and literature for many years. In my freshman writing courses, as in my advanced essay writing courses, I have to work hard to persuade students to move beyond surface observation. That is true even of the very strong students who are applying for scholarship opportunities.

These qualities combine to create difficulty for students attempting to write what they hope will be readable, insightful personal statements. Undoubtedly such statements are difficult for all writers; writing interestingly and engagingly about the self is an extraordinarily hard thing to do for young and old, for men and women. Adding to that difficulty is the fact that the typical writing prompt listed on the websites for major scholarships does not, and perhaps should not, provide much guidance.

Approaching the Personal Statement

Here is what one such website says about the personal statement required of applicants:

> *The* Personal Statement *should be a narrative giving a picture of you as an individual. Remember, applicants are not interviewed on the national level. The* Personal Statement *is your opportunity to "talk" about yourself and to tell the committee more about how you came to this point in your life and where you see yourself in the future. There is no single "right way" to approach the* Statement; *rather, each candidate will consider what they think is important for people reviewing the application to know about them.*
>
> *The* Statement *can deal with your personal history, family background, influences on your intellectual development, the educational and cultural opportunities (or lack of them) to which you have been exposed, and the ways in which these experiences have affected you. Also, you may include your special interests and abilities, career plans, and life goals, etc. It should*

> *not be a recording of facts already listed on the application or an elabora-*
> *tion of your Statement of Grant Purpose. It is more of an autobiography,*
> *and specifically related to you and your aspirations.*

For a young man or woman who is not particularly or exceptionally self-reflective—and that describes most young men and women, who envelop themselves in the present as a shield against the uncertain future—this is a daunting assignment. As a writing teacher, I can vouch for the fact that this well-meaning prompt, with its multiple options intended to open up at least one possibility for any conceivable applicant, will more likely cloud than illuminate the process of writing a powerful personal statement, for a number of reasons:

- The prompt's call for a narrative suggests a temporal organization; for young writers, that may mean a set of connectives: *and then, and then, and then.*

- Most college students, even gifted ones, arrive at this point in their lives simply by living, reacting each day to contingent circumstances; the strongest students among them are distinguished from the middling by their determined pursuit of excellence, not usually by detailed planning. But narratives, even autobiographical narratives, are not a natural fact—a simple, uncomplicated, unreflective record of what has happened—but rather a version of events for which writers selectively choose salient moments so as to construct a coherent story.

- It is very hard for inexperienced writers to know what insights reviewers are hoping to gain about them; it is hard for undergraduates to look at the world from the perspective of someone else, especially when that audience is anonymous.

- The first paragraph of the prompt quoted above encourages applicants to talk about themselves, noting that there is "no single 'right way' to approach the *Statement.*" The lack of a single "right way" is both liberating and frightening. If there is no right way, students are free to write anything. But if there is no right way, no method or template of the sort that years of learning to write essays for standardized tests and college applications have drummed into them, then how will they know what is effective?

- The second paragraph of the prompt cautions applicants to not simply list facts already included elsewhere in the application, and yet the multiple options suggested sequentially in the prompt— "your personal history, family background, influences on your intellectual development, the educational and cultural opportunities (or lack of them) to which you have been exposed, and the ways in which these experiences have affected you. . . . your special interests and abilities, career plans, and life goals, etc."—may well lure students into producing just such a list. (In fact, the warning against a simple "recording of facts" is there because the prompt itself seems to ask for one.) Even the well-meaning *etc.* at the end of the sequence is daunting, for it suggests that there are yet other experiences or accomplishments not explicitly mentioned that the applicant might wish or need to include.

To clarify for themselves what this prompt (or others like it) asks of them, applicants must do something that most have not been taught to do—they need to think rhetorically. That is, they must be aware that the personal statement is not an unmotivated narrative of the self but rather a situated text whose purpose is persuasive. The personal statement is not solely about themselves, and certainly not solely about themselves as isolate beings, though the label "personal statement" implies as much. An applicant must craft a rhetorically savvy narrative—please note, I do not mean insincere or untruthful or artificial—that persuades a particular set of reviewers for a particular scholarship of the particular applicant's quality and rightness for the scholarship. An applicant must write in such a way as to stand out from a crowd of similarly gifted applicants, without sounding boastful or falsely self-deprecating and without demeaning other applicants.

If all that is not complicated enough, here are some additional difficulties that hamper students who, once they understand the rhetorical dimensions of the task, labor to craft a persuasive personal statement:

- Most young people want to be like everyone else, not to be different from others. Or at least they want to be individual in the same way that everyone else is individual. But a good personal statement, like any engaging personal essay, requires a writer to explore himself or herself in careful detail and to cherish differences from as much as similarities to others.

- Inexperienced writers often believe that good writing results in a portable generalization—the moral of the story—that the reader can take away. Freshman writing is notorious for its omniscient tone and banal generalities. It is hard for inexperienced writers to resist the temptation to pronounce about self and world *ex cathedra.* But readers respond much less to overarching assertions of purpose or quality or moral conviction than they do to the particular details of lived experience. Any overarching assertions are best when they come at the end, after they have been earned, but even then such assertions need to be muted, need to be conclusions true to a particular experience rather than vaunting claims about human beings in all places and all times.

- Inexperienced writers often do not recognize what is valuable, that is to say, interesting, engaging, or emblematic of meaning in their own experience. Often to them, experience is a stream of undifferentiated events, so it is hard to focus on one or two such events as they flow by. For writers to focus on and develop one such experience, they must rescue it from the stream and observe it carefully. An inexperienced writer, who believes the interest and value of the event lie in the reductive lessons learned from it rather than in the event itself, is likely to focus on what *usually* or *typically* happens, rather than on something that is itself alone. In writing about a family reunion, for example, such writers might conflate ten annual reunions rather than focus on one, because they value experience in the aggregate rather than for its singularity.

- Because inexperienced writers "own" their particular memories, they forget that none of the rest of us knows the story. So when they hurry by a mention of a high school, a dog, a grandmother, or a trip to Geneva, they forget the reader does not know about these events. Writing that takes refuge in the general and denies us access to the particular is usually dead writing.

Exploring One's Life for Others

Writing prompts on the applications or websites for major scholarships do not, and perhaps should not, provide much guidance to the nervous applicant hoping to find clear direction for the writing task. After all, the primary purpose of scholarship foundations and agencies is not to teach promising young men and women to become successful candidates but rather to identify each year the best candidates for the scholarships. The role of fellowships advisors at colleges and universities, however, is different; it is the goal not merely to identify already superior candidates but also to foster promising young men and women who are in the process of discovering who they are and what their potential is. All of us encourage promising students to apply for competitive scholarships in the hope that they will grow to be among the fortunate ones to receive an award. But of course, inevitably, the majority of students who apply will not win awards, given the intense competition they face. So the value of applying must lie, for many, in something other than merely the award itself.

It is therefore important for us to stress the incalculable benefit *all* students stand to gain from the complex acts of introspection and analysis and composition that result in a high-quality scholarship application and in particular a well-wrought personal statement. Writing a powerful personal statement is not merely a technical task, not simply the tactical arrangement of words and sentences and paragraphs. An engaging personal statement is also not merely the result of a mysterious inspiration that exceeds altogether the reach of practical craft. Certainly it is not something that superior candidates naturally know how to produce. Instead, it is the conjunction of introspection and practical craft—along with an awareness of the rhetorical triad of writer, audience, and occasion—that results in a strong personal statement. Fellowships advisors cannot teach students to be self-aware any more than we can achieve for them excellence in and out of the classroom. But we can ask them questions, press for elaboration, encourage them to reach beyond the tried and true, the formulaic. We can help them to identify and articulate the strengths they harbor, sometimes without knowing it.

Let me close with some reflections written by a Hampden-Sydney student, a gifted young man who as a junior was a student in my creative nonfiction course and who subsequently completed an application for a competitive national scholarship and received the award. What follows is not a personal statement for a scholarship application but rather his conclusions about the value of exploring the self for others, as embodied in the portfolio of essays he wrote for my class. He put these insights to good use in the scholarship application he wrote the next semester:

This group of essays represents the first written reflections of my life. I have often read about, thought about, and talked about internal examination. However, before this portfolio, I had never written about it. I quickly learned about the difficulty of such an attempt. I faced the challenges that self-examination often brings about. I realized that when writing, I cannot just stop thinking when the topic becomes complex. The essay does not write itself. And unlike in academic pursuits, I met questions for which I simply do not know the answer, and I had no dictionary or textbook for reference. Neither Webster nor my course in macroeconomics can help me discover my purpose. . . . I love having the right answer all the time. In the process of writing, however, I learned that there are no right or wrong, black or white, yes or no answers to the questions of self-examination, regardless of my desire for them. . . . I have learned that the process of internal reflection is ongoing.

True, "the process of internal reflection is ongoing," but the task of writing a personal statement cannot go on forever. Deadlines are deadlines. But by encouraging able students to apply for competitive scholarships and thereby to confront their hopes and fears, their goals and ambitions, in the process of writing a meaningful personal statement, advisors can provide an educational experience of tremendous value in and of itself, whether or not the student wins an award.

Notes

1. Cashman's approach to "Helping Students to Tell Their Stories" is described in an article by James M. Lang that appeared in *The Chronicle of Higher Education* on 20 September 2012. Cashman also presented a version of his advice on the personal statement at the March 2012 NAFA workshop, "A Holistic Approach to Fellowships Advising," in Richmond, Virginia.

2. See https://www.e-education.psu.edu/writingrecommendationlettersonline/.

6

Bring Something Old, Learn Something New, Borrow a Lot, and Conduct an Analytical Review

DOUG CUTCHINS

Doug Cutchins is the director of global awards at New York University Abu Dhabi. Previously, he was the director of social commitment, and then associate dean and director of postgraduate transitions at Grinnell College, positions that he held for a total of fifteen years. Cutchins served in the leadership of NAFA as a member of the board of directors from 2005 to 2009, then as vice president from 2009 to 2011, and president from 2011 to 2013. He also coauthored four editions of the book Volunteer Vacations: Short-Term Adventures That Will Benefit You and Others, *and served on the board and as president of both the Grinnell-Newburg (Iowa) School District and the Grinnell, Iowa, United Way. He is a returned Peace Corps volunteer (Suriname, 1995–97), and holds an MA in history from the University of Connecticut and a BA in history with secondary teaching licensure from Grinnell College.*

L ike many NAFA members, I never set out to become a fellowships advisor and had little direct experience in the field when I was hired for my first fellowships advising job at Grinnell College in 1999. I dove into the job head first, not knowing a Marshall from a Rhodes, nor a Fulbright from a Watson. Over the fifteen years that I worked at Grinnell, and in no small part due to my association with NAFA, I learned a tremendous amount about our profession, figured out how to do my work more and more effectively, and improved as a fellowships advisor.

In time, I was successful at my work, and the number of students who considered or actually did apply for fellowships at Grinnell increased markedly. We had our fair share of students who received awards, and—crucially—students understood and appreciated the value of the process.

While I was happy, overall, with the state of developing a culture of fellowships advising and applications at Grinnell, a number of questions lurked in the back of my mind: What could we or should we be doing differently? What decisions or assumptions had I made long ago that I never questioned, or that still had an impact on my work? If I could go back to 1999 and keep my fifteen years of experience, what would I do differently?

We rarely if ever get do-overs in our lives. But, in a sense, that is what I was able to do in 2014 when I changed fellowships advising jobs, moving from the cornfields of Iowa to the sand dunes of Abu Dhabi. I left a fifteen-year-old office at the first college established west of the Mississippi for New York University Abu Dhabi (NYUAD), a four-year-old institution that had no formal fellowships advising office. I was faced, once again, with a blank slate on which I could design my own fellowships program, but this time I was armed with the knowledge my work at Grinnell and with NAFA had given me.

That is not to say that I was eager to leave Grinnell. After fifteen years (plus four years in a previous stint as an undergrad there), that little town on the prairie sure felt like home; my family and I were settled there and were not looking to leave. I had often joked that it was going to take a crowbar to get us out of there. And while there were personal reasons behind this big decision—chief among them the chance to raise our children internationally and send them to a world-class school—the professional opportunities at NYUAD were the main impetus pushing me to make this leap.

NYUAD has three main features that make it an attractive professional opportunity. The first is the students who attend the school. NYUAD likes to call itself "the world's honors college." Students come from a stunning array of countries, with no country represented by more than 20 percent of the student body. With need-blind admissions and generous financial aid packages, including a no-loan policy, the university seeks to enroll the very best students in the world, regardless of their ability to pay. That has led to an incredible pool of applicants, one of the lowest acceptance rates in the world (under 5 percent), and an academically stellar student body. I have sometimes said that fellowships advisors are like sculptors: we are only as good as our clay. NYUAD has exceptionally good clay.

Second, the university was eager to prioritize fellowships advising in Abu Dhabi. As a new, high-visibility project, the larger NYU administration based in Washington Square was eager to have traditional markers of success to demonstrate the excellence of the NYUAD student body and its experiences. They already had some positive results before I arrived, as one American student in the first graduating class had received both a Truman and a U.S. Rhodes Scholarship, and two other NYUAD students were the first recipients of the newly created Falcon Scholarship, which is now the UAE Rhodes Scholarship, a project of the Rhodes Trust for United Arab Emirates (UAE) college graduates from non-Rhodes-eligible countries. These successes and the university's subsequent enthusiasm were a double-edged sword for me. They helped pave a path and generate enthusiasm for the endeavor, but I needed to reorient some definitions of "success" to include students who did not receive awards but whose lives were deeply affected by the process of applying for them.

The third highly attractive piece of moving to Abu Dhabi was the chance to start a new office from scratch once again. Now that I not only knew the differences between Marshall and Rhodes and Fulbright and Watson but also knew them in painstaking detail, I had the chance to focus my work from day one on developing scholars rather than on developing scholarship applicants. It freed me to start not at the starting line from a dead standstill, as I had previously, but with a lead and a full head of steam.

That is not to say that my new position is the same job as I had at Grinnell, nor that I have not had a lot to learn. In fact, one of the most surprising things has been how little of the specific knowledge about scholarship programs I brought with me has actually translated to Abu Dhabi.

I know the difference between a Rhodes and a Marshall, but that does not do me much good since NYUAD students—even the Americans—are ineligible for the Marshall Scholarship, since they are not educated in the United States. And being able to tease out subtle nuances to determine whether a student is a better fit for Fulbright or Watson does not help much when 80 percent of our students are not eligible for the U.S. Fulbright Student Program, and NYUAD is not a Watson-eligible school.

The NYUAD students are also significantly different from Grinnell students. During my interview process, I had to pause whenever I tried to describe how internationalized Grinnell is. While it is quite internationalized for a typical U.S. institution, with 60 percent of the students studying abroad, and 13 percent of the student body coming from other countries, those numbers are dwarfed by NYUAD's student body, all of whom study abroad (80 percent do so for two terms), and for most the very experience of studying in Abu Dhabi already constitutes an international and certainly intercultural experience. One of the biggest challenges—and most exciting developments—for me in this new position has been learning how to advise scholarship candidates across cultural boundaries. I have conversations daily with students who have very different views from those I hold about the influence of family members on life choices, the role of prestige and money versus passion and interest, the challenges of visas and passports, and concepts of the value of a liberal arts education. None of these conversations are easy or comfortable, but they are interesting and important.

Working with this different student body has also forced a change in my roster of scholarships and brought a slew of new awards into my consciousness. Some awards have left my sphere of work, such as the previously mentioned Marshall and Watson along with Gilman and Critical Languages Scholarships, among others, due to eligibility requirements. Others remain but with caveats: chief among these are the many awards that restrict eligibility to U.S. citizens, since that slice of the population makes up a minority of NYUAD students. Still, we would be silly to completely ignore U.S.-citizen-only awards like the Truman or U.S. Fulbright or Goldwater or others, given the importance those hold to students and their future careers.

But added to those awards that I am used to are a whole new list of awards that I have perhaps heard of but never worked with before, such as DAAD and Erasmus Mundus, and an even longer list of awards that I am discovering for the first time, including the Swiss Government Award, the Mandela-Rhodes, the Commonwealth Scholarships, and the Open Society Civil Leadership Award. (See also the addendum to this piece, "Four New Ones," for a discussion of four awards that are not highly promoted by U.S. fellowships advisors but should be.) What is interesting, as I learn about these, is that I have a feeling of starting over, of returning to 1999 and learning, wide-eyed, the basics of what these awards are, whom they seek to fund, and how their application processes work. The difference, though, is that I feel I have a more solid base from which to ask these questions and understand the answers. I know what to look for and how to interpret what I am told. I may be crossing unfamiliar terrain with these awards, but I feel like I am already able to do so at a jogging pace.

The biggest lesson I learned from my work at Grinnell, and something I have been demonstrably loud about preserving in Abu Dhabi, is a need to limit the scope of the work that I do. Starting at Grinnell, I not only had little idea what these awards were but had even less of a sense of what it would take to do the job of recruiting students, supporting them, and administering the processes. Over the course of fifteen years, the job grew (I should rephrase that in an active voice to take responsibility and blame for that, actually: "*I* grew the job . . .") to an almost unmanageable beast of a portfolio, large enough that it had to be split into two full-time jobs when I departed. I loved my work at Grinnell, but it was overwhelming me by the time I left and was impeding my ability to be effective in all aspects of my work.

Arriving in Abu Dhabi gave me a chance to correct this long-term mistake and to define the scholarships advising work I do in a narrow enough way to be successful in the long-term. From the beginnings of my interviews here, I pitched the idea of creating a "Roster of 40," a curated list of forty awards chosen to meet the specific talents, strengths, and demographic challenges of the NYUAD student body. Virtually all of my work would be focused on the awards on this roster; while I would be happy to work with and advise students who were applying for opportunities not on the Roster of 40, I would not recruit nor actively seek to advise applicants for these awards.

In doing so, I was simply formalizing a process that all NAFA members go through. I do not think that any NAFA member claims that they work with all awards. A quick scan of any of the major online scholarship databases turns up thousands, if not tens of thousands, of scholarships, fellowships, awards, and grants. One person or office cannot know about, let alone become an expert on or recruit for, all of those awards. We all necessarily limit our work in some way. At Grinnell, I had made my own "roster" by happenstance, inheriting a list that existed before I arrived, picking up others at NAFA conferences or from the listserv, adding some when a faculty member forwarded me an email from a foundation with a note that said, "We really should encourage our students to apply for this!" or by any of the dozens of other ways that an opportunity might come across my radar. In doing so, though, I lacked strategy and direction. If I had been challenged to explain why some awards were on my roster instead of the thousands that were not, I would have been hard-pressed to give a cogent and coherent answer.

Creating NYUAD's Roster of 40 was a chance to press the reset button and to approach what I would argue is one of our most important tasks as scholarships advisors—defining what we do and do not do—with a greater sense of purpose. In doing so, I had to take into account the makeup, culture, demographics, and likely plans of our student body (and develop a sense of these quickly), combined with institutional priorities and expectations, and my own base of knowledge. The Madison Fellowship, for example, is an unlikely yet solid entry on the NYUAD Roster of 40. Given its narrow focus and U.S. citizenship restriction, NYUAD would be unlikely, in most cases, to include it, except that my previous experience as a selection committee member for the Madison makes it easier for me to recruit and advise students. My supervisor and I also agreed from the start that the Roster of 40 would be a living list and that we would feel free, as we have already begun doing, to add and subtract awards from it as our student body changes, as awards change, and as our own institutional priorities change.

Several other challenges awaited me in Abu Dhabi, not all of which I had anticipated. First among those was needing to prove myself all over again. After fifteen years at Grinnell, I was pretty deeply ingrained into the culture of that small institution; several people told me as I left that they just assumed I was a lifer there, holding some form of administrative tenure. Grinnell's scholarship successes meant that I had a certain level of credibility with faculty, students, and colleagues, none of which traveled in my suitcases with me to the UAE. Upon arriving, I had to start building trust from scratch, convincing my peers, the students, and the faculty that I had some sense of what I was doing. I mostly approached this task in my first six months through hard work, which made me happier than ever to have the buffer of the Roster of 40 to be able to logically resist work that fell outside the list.

Another challenge I had not anticipated was to create the workings of the office anew. So much of what I relied on in my day-to-day work at Grinnell—the unthinking gear shifts of the mechanism of advising—I had built slowly over time. Faculty committees, calendars, nomination processes, presidential signatures on letters of nominations, waiver statements, even relationships with key players like the registrar were all just in the air around me, requiring little work to maintain. It is easy to forget, after so many years doing this work, how much goes into our work . . . until creating all of it anew, in a new context, is necessary.

A final challenge is a new twist on my work, incorporating elements I have never had to think about previously. NYUAD is a part of New York University proper; it is not structured as a separate or branch campus but instead as an "alternate location" of NYU, and our students are treated as the students of any other school of NYU. When it comes to Truman nominations, for example, NYU as a whole—including our students in New York, Abu Dhabi, and (soon) Shanghai—has four nominations total, not four nominations per campus. This means that I have needed to work in close collaboration with colleagues nine time zones away, including a supervisor who provides general direction for my work, and NYU's scholarship director, Jenni Quilter. She came into her job at the same time I did, in summer 2014, so together we have been navigating the landscape of this new relationship and partnership. We have had to figure out joint nomination processes, how to select nominees across continents, put together committees of faculty members from both campuses, figure out how to communicate together with foundations, and coordinate messaging and administration. It has not been an easy task and requires weekly hour-long Skype conversations and near-daily emails. I have also had to learn how to share my work and give up control of certain aspects, as I have never had a colleague that I have partnered with as much as I do now. But, in much more than an equal trade, I have also learned so much from finally (finally!) having a collaborator, compatriot, and sounding board.

One of the greatest benefits of making this change has been learning how much it helps to have someone to provide a different perspective and to get me out of my own echo chamber of advising.

Not everything has been new and different. I found quite a few skills and bases of knowledge that I was able to unpack, dust off, welcome to Abu Dhabi, and quickly put to use. Fulbright ETA candidates are Fulbright ETA candidates, regardless of whether they are in Iowa or Abu Dhabi. The nuances of each student are different, but overall, I know what I am doing with Fulbright, even here in Abu Dhabi. Similarly, I know how to advise a student about a personal statement, and the basics of my style and temperament in working with students have remained relatively constant, even as the students I am working with have changed considerably. Many of my resources about how to obtain letters of recommendation and how to approach a personal statement have carried over, almost untouched (though I did rewrite the intro to the personal statement handout, given that it started with Supreme Court Justice Potter Stewart's famous statement about pornography: "I know it when I see it," which I applied to high-quality personal statements. Local sensibilities being what they are here, I thought that paragraph needed a rewrite.)

Six months after landing in Abu Dhabi, I am feeling relatively settled in my work. I have my Roster of 40 completed, we have made it through our first round of applications, and we have had success in both traditional and nontraditional ways, as students begin to grasp the benefits of the process. Jenni Quilter and I are into a rhythm and have figured out some of the nuances of Skype. I have a website up and running, waiver forms approved, and am beginning to be known on campus. I am hoping that we can now start to build the stuff of scholarships advising dreams: a true scholar development program, systematic processes for identifying and cultivating talent, and using fellowship application processes as a way to inspire students to heights of achievement that they might not otherwise have sought. The prospects are exciting.

Finally, what lessons can other advisors learn from my experiences? For veteran advisors, it is relatively simple: don't be afraid to shake up routines. Jumping from Grinnell was scary and difficult but ultimately proved to be a worthwhile and rewarding move, one that taught me a lot about how I do my job, allowed me to reinvent my processes and question my actions, and energized me by forcing me to learn new aspects of my work. For newer advisors, the lesson may be a bit broader: this is hard work, even for those of us who have been doing it for some time. The learning curve is steep, and a good amount of background work goes into establishing a reputation and an office. Lastly, it is important to be careful and intentional in defining the work, recognizing that limits have to be set for the work to be manageable and for students to fully benefit.

Addendum: Four New Ones

Let's face it: there are awards we all work with because it is expected that we do so. There are awards that we usually work with. There are awards we think we should work with more than we do, or that we would work more on if extra hours were added to the day.

But there are also awards that, I would guess, very few to none of us work on but that are remarkable opportunities and are available to a large percentage of our students. These all allow U.S. citizens to apply and do not have a list of institutions that are allowed to nominate. They are hidden gems, not quite undiscovered, but certainly not talked about nearly as much as many of their peers.

I have been learning about these in the 2014–15 academic year because my job requires me to do so. Moving to New York University's new campus in Abu Dhabi brought me in contact with a hugely different range of students. Gone were the days when I could blithely assume that my students wanted to attend graduate school in the United States (or, for the adventurous, the UK) or take on a one-year Fulbright stint. I could no longer assume that my students would be U.S. citizens, since 80 percent of NYUAD's students do not fall into that demographic. To do my job well, I was forced to look outside of what I have come to think of as the NAFA Comfort Zone of scholarships and fellowships, and to start discovering a range of awards that might lead our students to unexpected and new places.

And, like any good NAFA member, I did not want to keep this information to myself. Below are four hidden gems—awards that are probably on all our databases somewhere—that most of us have likely spent little to no time working on but deserve much more attention than they are getting. As always with any written publication like this, please confirm all information on the awards' websites, as these awards change and alter their details over time.

Endeavor Scholarships

https://aei.gov.au/Scholarships-and-Fellowships/Pages/default.aspx

Endeavor Scholarships are relatively unknown in the United States. Several awards exist under the general Endeavor umbrella, but all include generous funding for study, research, or other academic ventures in Australia (or for Australians to undertake elsewhere). The Australian government provides funding for these awards, which fund around five hundred students per year. Awards include a travel stipend, establishment allowance, monthly stipend, health insurance, and tuition benefits (which may not cover all costs). Students can enroll in a two-year MA or four-year PhD program, either by course work or research (following the British model). Research fellowships allow for four-to-six-month research projects in Australia for students enrolled in non-Australian graduate degree programs. Endeavor also offers vocational and executive training programs. Applications are online, and the competition opens annually in April. Some programs require an offer of admission before the student may apply for the Endeavor Scholarship. Endeavor Scholars are expected to return to their home country at the conclusion of their studies. While the list of countries of origin for candidates is extensive (and includes the United States), it is not all-encompassing.

Japanese Government Scholarship

http://www.mext.go.jp/a_menu/koutou/ryugaku/boshu/1346643.htm

The plain-text, detail-oriented website for the Japanese Government Scholarship is about the only thing not exciting about this unique and again not-as-well-known award. Funded by the Japanese Ministry of Education, Culture, Sports, Science, and Technology, the Japanese Government Scholarship provides funding for students from countries that have diplomatic relations with Japan, either for nondegree or enrolled graduate studies. Most fields are allowed, though there are restrictions in the health sciences and, interestingly, traditional Japanese arts such as Kabuki theater. Candidates do not have to speak Japanese but must be willing and enthusiastic about learning Japanese language and culture; students who do not speak Japanese will enroll in a six-month introductory course upon arrival. Grants are typically eighteen to twenty-four months, and include a monthly allowance, travel costs, and full tuition. Selection is made by the diplomatic mission in the student's home country, after which time the Japanese government assists with placing the recipients in appropriate universities.

Organization of American States (OAS) Regular Program for Academic Scholarships (Graduate)

http://www.oas.org/en/scholarships/regular_program.asp

The Organization of American States (OAS) has a terrific program that allows students from member states—including the United States—to study at other universities in the OAS. This is a terrific opportunity for students who are competing for those tough-to-get Fulbright grants to seek other ways to pursue their study plans. Candidates must be enrolled in a full-time, degree-seeking program, and funding lasts for up to two years. Scholars' studies must be related to one of the eight OAS development goals: broadly speaking, these are social development, education, economic diversification, scientific development, democratization, sustainable tourism, environmental sustainability, and culture (see details of each of these on the OAS website). Interestingly, whereas some grants require students to return to their home countries, the OAS grant requires recipients to stay in their host country for a minimum of two years after their studies are complete. Candidates can apply either to a preselected "Consortium University," which increases their chances of receiving the award, or go for a more competitive open placement slot. OAS scholarship recipients receive airfare, tuition, a books allowance, health insurance, and a monthly allowance. The deadline for U.S. citizens is typically in April.

Swiss Government Excellence Scholarships

http://www.sbfi.admin.ch

The Swiss government offers a massive and multifaceted scholarship program to bring in students from around the world to study in Switzerland. U.S. citizens are not a focus of this program but are eligible for two of the grants offered: Fine Arts Scholarships and Research Scholarships. Fine Arts Scholarships are available for students of all artistic disciplines at selected Swiss universities, leading to a master's degree. Candidates must be under thirty-five years old and must have completed their BA within the past three years. Admission at the student's chosen institution is a separate process from the scholarship application. The Research Scholarships are post-PhD or post-MD grants, offered at a wide range of Swiss universities, are for twelve months, and are nonrenewable. Candidates for the Research Scholarships must also be under thirty-five years old and must have a letter from a Swiss researcher offering to supervise the postdoctoral research. Both awards include a stipend, health insurance, airfare, housing, and other limited benefits. The awards are administered in the United States by IIE, and applications are usually due in October.

While we all have our comfort zones in scholarships advising that allow us to build a level of expertise and excellence in our work, it is also helpful and healthy for us each to continue to grow and push the boundaries of that comfort zone. By presenting NAFA members with four new awards (that may not be familiar to all) that many of our students will be eligible for, I hope I am encouraging all of us to keep digging for (and sharing) new opportunities and, ultimately, to connect even more outstanding young scholars to new international experiences.

7

Workshops That Attract and Engage Students

MONIQUE BOURQUE, LAURA COTTEN, AND BECKY MENTZER

Monique Bourque is director of Health Professions Advising and Student Fellowships at Willamette University and holds an adjunct appointment in the Environmental and Earth Sciences Department. She received her master's and doctoral degrees in American history and museum studies from the Hagley Fellows program at the University of Delaware. Previously she was fellowships and prizes advisor at Swarthmore College, an assistant dean for postbaccalaureate programs in the College of General Studies at the University of Pennsylvania, and an archivist at several historical libraries in the Philadelphia area. She has served on a range of national scholarship committees. She has published in academic journals, including the Journal of the Early Republic, *and in edited collections, including NAFA's* All In: Expanding Access through Nationally Competitive Awards *(2013).*

Laura Cotten *is the associate director for Fellowship and Graduate School Advising at the University of Dayton. She is located in the University Honors Program but works with the entire student population, to include graduate students. Previously she worked for the Franklin W. Olin College of Engineering as the first assistant director for Admission and Post-Graduate Planning, establishing the fellowships office. Cotten holds a master of education from the College of William and Mary and a bachelor of science in anthropology from James Madison University.*

Becky Mentzer *recently retired from Illinois State University, where she served as the Honors Program associate director, coordinator of the Presidential Scholars Program, and the Fulbright Program advisor. She currently is enjoying semiretirement with a private practice doing professional development workshops and career counseling. Mentzer participated in NAFA New Advisor workshops and served on panels at various NAFA conferences. She also cochaired the Major Scholarships Committee of the National Collegiate Honors Council and provided training to advisors and students through NCHC conference presentations. Mentzer earned a BS and MS in psychology from Illinois State University and holds a license as a clinical professional counselor.*

Engaging students in learning about fellowships is often a difficult process. Top students at a university, who often make the best candidates, are already busy with class work, internships, and cocurricular activities. Most students, staff, and faculty are not sure what the word *fellowships* even means. How then do we not only find the top students on our university campuses to apply for prestigious fellowships but also convince them that this is an excellent use of their already scarce time? Developing innovative methods for reaching students is vital to a successful fellowships office.

This essay describes different tactics for reaching and then engaging students who will make excellent scholarship candidates. The first meets students where they are and so includes social media. We all know the impact students can have on one another. The same advice given by a fellowships advisor means much less than that advice coming from a peer. Enlisting the help of previous recipients of prestigious fellowships can be an effective way to show students the benefits of applying. We must value the time of our students. Another approach is to organize presentations by specialty sessions to ensure students understand the breadth of awards available to their particular discipline or area of interest. When speaking in classrooms or with students in a variety of majors, it is not always possible to know the fields of interest for all students. In these circumstances another tactic is to involve students in a fellowships activity to increase interest and maintain attention for the entire length of the presentation. The following examples have been used at various campuses and have been found to be successful in attracting and engaging students in the fellowship process.

Including Successful Peers as Speakers

Teaching one-hour honors interdisciplinary classes based on various themes creates an opportunity to have guest lectures on the topic. For instance, a psychology professor who studies false memories for a class titled "A Trip Down Memory Lane," and a nursing professor who researches sleep and students for "Sleep, Dreams and the Unconscious" are examples of highly rated class sessions. Why not apply this approach to scholarship workshops?

Interesting speakers who are experts in various aspects of the scholarship process can address potential applicants providing a different perspective, complementing the scholarships advisor's role of presenting the nuts and bolts. The advisor becomes the process expert and even cheerleader for special opportunities, but those who have applied successfully have the experience that makes them the experts from an audience perspective. Students thinking of applying enjoy hearing about firsthand experiences. Below are three ways to include previous recipients in the student recruitment process.

Connecting in person: It is always helpful to get peers involved who can share their experiences with the application process at campus information meetings. Former or current scholars can be the best advocates for a program because of what they have learned in the process of applying. Having Goldwater Scholars, Critical Language Scholars, US-UK Fulbright Summer Institute Scholars, and Fulbright U.S. Student Scholars (or alternates or honorable mentions) speak can have a powerful impact on students attending the meeting. For example, asking a Fulbright Scholar who successfully negotiated the application process for a research grant to talk about arranging an affiliation can help students understand what is sometimes a complicated process. Faculty members should also be encouraged to attend and to share how important networking can be to the process of finding an affiliation.

Students recognized at the national level who are still on campus or in the area can participate in person. But workshops for Fulbright, Rhodes, Marshall, Gates, Truman, and so on are still possible using any one of many forms of social media, even when successful candidates are off participating in internships, attending graduate school abroad, or teaching through one of those nationally competitive scholarships.

Using Skype: For example, Bill, a successful Fulbright grant recipient, was in Moldova researching microfinance institutions. Even though the time difference was seven hours, he was willing to stay up to talk with workshop participants. With his appearance publicized in advance, the workshop was well attended. Bill was engaging and informative, explaining how he made decisions and why it was important to him to have assistance from his scholarships advisor and his professors. He talked about arranging an affiliation and what his experience was like throughout the process at home and later in Moldova. He spoke for about fifteen minutes before signing off, and the Fulbright workshop presentation continued. Evaluations showed it was very effective.

Using YouTube: Jessica, who enjoyed a Fulbright ETA in Montenegro, had such a life-changing experience that she pursued another program, teaching English in Romania. She was interested in talking about her Fulbright experience but less eager to stay up until two o'clock in the morning to do it. She created a ten-minute video to be included at an informational workshop. She spoke about how she selected Montenegro, what her experiences had been that made her competitive, and what it was like to be responsible for an English classroom at the university level as an ETA. This feature of the workshop was advertised broadly and attracted a number of students who were interested in an ETA and in learning more about Jessica's experiences. Some students were interested in the current competitions, and some were simply looking to the future, assessing what the expectations would be. A twist on a standard practice made this a very effective workshop, and the video became a link on that institution's scholarships website for future ETA applicants to watch.

Specialty Sessions: Organizing Program Information according to Interests and Goals

Every institution has programs that are important to it because of an especially strong record or the association of the award with a particular student, and most advisors facilitate information sessions that focus specifically on those programs. Even though these sessions can result in a substantial number of applicants for headliner programs like Truman or Fulbright, focusing on these programs may not be the best way to reach the broadest range of students or to respond effectively to the shifting needs or developing strengths of particular student populations. It may be helpful to develop a range of information sessions in addition to the "headliners" that are organized around students' goals and interests and focus on a range of other programs, like those that fund study in the UK. Useful meetings could also include STEM scholarships meetings for seniors that focus on the National Science Foundation's Graduate Research Fellowships Program, and Department of Defense and National Defense Science and Engineering Graduate fellowships. This programming flexibility allows advisors to respond more nimbly to the concerns of students, can be useful in supporting the priorities of the fellowships advisor or office, and can remind an institution's faculty and higher administration of the ways in which the office contributes to the institution's mission.

RESPONDING TO STUDENTS' NEEDS AND CONCERNS

The two most intractable problems in student outreach are connecting with students who do not see themselves as candidates for high-profile scholarships like the Truman, Goldwater, or Fulbright, and overcoming students' "received wisdom" about what certain scholarship programs require or prefer in their applicants. Often these two problems are intertwined. Many advisors hear about students whose peers have informed them that the Fulbright grants are only for research and the program prefers the sciences, or about excellent potential Truman candidates who did not plan to apply (or, worse, who watched the deadline go by) because they are confident their GPAs are too low and their service experiences are not strong enough. Or potential candidates may have decided that the program is only for those planning on careers in politics or the law. These students may not attend program information sessions because of misinformation, never realizing that they could be competitive.

We are not recommending eliminating individual information sessions for programs that typically require a great deal of information sharing at the beginning of the process and for whom a school may have large applicant pools, like the Fulbright. However, organizing additional information sessions around interests that these programs address can both help an advisor present students with a wider range of options in addition to these programs, and give that advisor the opportunity to correct students' misconceptions about the programs. At one institution, for example, over a period of several years attendance at Truman information sessions was extremely low even when the advisor promoted them heavily and had a current scholar there to answer questions and discuss her experience (usually a surefire draw), and the applicant pool was both small and disturbingly shallow.

When the advisor organized a session around programs for students interested in social justice—a big issue for many students—the room was full, and the advisor was able to showcase programs like PPIA and the Emerson Hunger Fellowship, and training opportunities like those offered by the Drum Major Institute, with the result that the university had applicants for these programs for the first time in several years. Even better, the advisor was able to connect with students who had not been thinking about the fellowships office as a potential resource for them, because they did not believe there was any organizational funding for social justice work.

Planning sessions that showcase a number of goal-oriented programs can be helpful in identifying and overcoming problems with the comfortable patterns of outreach that an advisor may have developed over time. One advisor watched in dismay as attendance at information sessions about the Udall scholarship declined to a trickle over several years, until finally a current Udall scholar shone a light on the problem by asking about the office hosting a session about programs for students interested in environmental issues. The advisor's promotional efforts for the Udall had always presented a view of both wings of the program: Native American health issues and tribal policy, and environmental issues. The scholar recounted a conversation with a classmate who was reluctant to attend the meeting despite an abiding interest in environmental issues. The classmate explained that he had deleted the advisor's emails about the program and not attended the information session because he "didn't know anything" about Native American health issues or tribal policy. In addition to underscoring the value of a session that covers a range of programs for students interested in environmental issues, the advisor was encouraged to think carefully about segmenting emails to the appropriate audiences, stressing Udall as environmental programs to the appropriate group and Native American policy to another. This insight will help that advisor think and work more creatively and collaboratively with staff on outreach efforts that target specific audiences.

Focusing and refocusing on students' broader needs can allow advisors to identify new areas where they can contribute to the efforts of other offices on campus and contribute to the university's mission in creative ways. The current landscape of financial aid, for example, is changing rapidly, and many of our institutions are not as effective as we would like to be in supporting first-generation and low-income students and their families. At some institutions, there is often a substantial difference for students in the financial aid package between first and second years, and advisors may see increasing numbers of students who cannot afford to return for sophomore year. At one institution, the director of the financial aid office and the fellowships advisor have begun conducting workshops in the upcoming fall and spring for first-year students focused on financial aid planning and strategies for identifying and applying for scholarships in time to obtain assistance for the second year of college and beyond. They hope that proactive programming like this will have a positive effect on retention rates.

NETWORKING WITH FACULTY

At any institution, the role of the faculty in identifying strong student candidates and encouraging them to apply is crucial in developing competitive applicant pools. Maintaining the network of positive relationships with faculty, which makes referrals easy and support of applicants straightforward, can be a substantial effort. Providing materials (like handouts) for goal- or discipline-focused information sessions to appropriate faculty can develop and promote these relationships and supply faculty with materials for their own reference and for handing to students during advising appointments. Advisor visits to departmental meetings can be an opportunity to connect with new faculty in particular, and focused information sessions conducted for specific departments can be useful in reaching both students and faculty—presentations on language study and study-abroad programs for Russian and German, for example. Faculty can make as many false assumptions as students do about what a particular program is for or what the program prefers. Interactions during sessions like these and during departmental meetings can be low-stress opportunities to correct misconceptions and answer questions about both fellowships and the fellowships office.

These interactions are also an excellent way to educate new faculty about the scholarship application process. Many of us already regularly conduct sessions for faculty on issues like writing recommendation letters, but talking to faculty in smaller groups about their students' needs, interests, and academic issues can provide a valuable perspective on the work and help advisors stay flexible in our thinking about programming and relationships with both students and faculty.

The constant turnover in faculty through retirements, new hires, and the use of adjuncts, coupled with the fact that scholarship availability and application requirements change over time, means that relationships with faculty need nearly constant tending in order to be effective. The benefit of this work is that robust faculty relationships contribute to stronger and more diverse applicant pools and to better awareness on campus of the scholarships office's efforts and functions. In addition, stronger relationships with faculty make managing the application process less onerous for the fellowships advisor in negotiating suggested revisions to recommendation letters, motivating faculty to meet deadlines, and convincing faculty to serve on interview panels or committees.

STRATEGIC PLANNING AND PROFESSIONAL FLEXIBILITY

Developing information sessions with the goal of responding to shifts in the demographic characteristics or interests of the students at an institution can offer opportunities for effective collaboration with other offices and for relationship building with new staff positions and new staff members in existing offices. Administrative reorganization at one institution recently opened a position in vocational discernment in the career services offices for a staff member who had been doing this work through an internal grant program. This staff member and the fellowships advisor developed and conducted a workshop for students on moving from the process of values identification and goal formation to making a plan for pursuing those goals through postgraduate work or in applications to graduate or professional school. Workshop attendance was low, but the presenters received positive feedback, and they will be offering it again. Programs like this one allow us to think more creatively than we otherwise might about outreach and service to students. If an institution's strategic plan includes a goal that each student graduates with a career plan, collaborations like this also allow both offices to contribute to the goal and to underscore their value to the institution.

Making it a goal to think regularly about collaboration with staff in other offices and to reach out to students in new ways requires frequent review of available programs and their changing requirements but will be a tremendous aid in avoiding burnout. Personal satisfaction and the range and number of scholarship applications are all likely to increase.

Active Student Engagement during Presentations

Undergraduates today are busier than ever when it comes to classes, research, internships, and studying abroad. Although these activities make a student's time scarce, they also create excellent fellowship candidates. New advisors too often present information about different awards in a lecture-style format, convinced that the amounts of money available or the opportunity to engage in a graduate degree will hold their attention. Too often this is not the case. Some advisors have used an engaging activity-styled approach, shared through NAFA. This activity is best used with a small group of students, no more than fifteen, and with students who know one another. If the students are unfamiliar with each other, an icebreaker will allow students to become better acquainted. This approach can also be modified for larger groups who may or may not know one another.

SMALL GROUPS

Find an existing group of high-caliber students already formed at the institution. For example, some institutions may have an honors program or honors college that encourages students to complete a thesis. Engage a group of these students in professional development. If there are a number of thesis writers, divide the writers into smaller groups of ten to fifteen based on their field of study. This will also enable the fellowships advisor to adjust the fellowships discussed to better fit the group of students present.

To begin this activity, create at least fourteen different posters with descriptions of the top fellowship opportunities. Although there may be additional fellowships available, the purpose of this activity is to get students excited about the potential of fellowships and seek out others that may also suit their career paths. Create twenty-two case scenarios corresponding with the posters. The size of the group of students will determine how many scenarios each student will receive. Then instruct students that they are to select which fellowships their student profile best matches. Students then walk around the room, read about the different fellowships, and select from the posters present. Keep the scenarios vague enough that each profile matches with more than one fellowship. This requires students to look longer at the different options and increases the chance they will become interested in specific awards themselves as well. After allowing roughly fifteen or twenty minutes for students to come up with answers, reconvene the group. Have each student read aloud the case scenario and comment about which award or awards the student should consider applying to in the future. With the introduction of a new award, the advisor can discuss the award in brief, giving additional details and telling the stories of university students who may have won that particular award. The end of the session can be used to determine which awards students are interested in applying for later in their undergraduate careers.

LARGER GROUPS

For larger groups, the same case scenario event can be used. Create a PowerPoint with the case scenarios rather than handing out cards. Hang the same posters around the room in a manner where students can view them from their seats. As a group, discuss the basics of fellowships for the first ten to fifteen minutes. Select students from the audience to read aloud the case scenario currently in view on the PowerPoint. Someone in the group will then determine for which awards the student profile is a good candidate. Calling on a student to read the case scenario aloud and then asking the group to decide which award is appropriate for this individual is often successful. In a larger group decrease the number of case scenarios, and discuss each award in detail as it is selected. Larger groups generally tend to be in classes with a specific field of study in mind. By using this information to structure the presentation, the students will develop a better understanding about what each award has to offer. It is important to respect the time of students and know the audience. Do not flood students with information that is not useful, with information about applications when deadlines have passed, or with information about programs with high standards not likely to be met by those in the audience.

Conclusion: Don't Get Set in Your Ways!

There are many ways to engage students in the fellowship process. Do not hesitate to ask or survey applicants about which outreach efforts have been most effective in their individual experiences, and use their comments in stepping back to rethink programming each year. Enlisting students as volunteers (past applicants who have been through the experience of applying, current scholars abroad willing to connect remotely via Skype or YouTube) will enliven presentations. Keeping information relevant to students and ensuring that the time spent discussing awards is used properly is also important. Holding field-specific information sessions will help attract the right students, and engaging them in small or large groups with hands-on activities will increase retention about the awards discussed. Sharing case scenarios and telling stories about students from the institution who have been successful in winning fellowships will make the audience feel as though they too can be competitive.

Part III

The Advisor Toolkit

8

More Connected? Implications of Information and Communication Technology for Fellowships Advising

JENNIFER GERZ-ESCANDÓN

Jennifer Gerz-Escandón is the director of national scholarships and fellowships for the Georgia State University Honors College. Her previous roles include associate professor and chair of international relations and director of the Center for International Programs and Services at Lynn University. Prior to Lynn, she held the position of director of international studies and assistant professor of political science at the University of Evansville. A highlight of her more than a dozen years in higher education was a 2001–2 International Education Administrator Fulbright experience in Germany. Gerz-Escandón is advisor to the Gates Millennium Scholarship Georgia State chapter and regularly serves as a scholarship reader for the Congressional Hispanic Caucus Institute Scholarship Program and the Asian Pacific Islander American Scholarship Fund. She holds a BA in government with a minor in psychology from Georgetown University, an MA in international relations from the University of Miami, a postgraduate diploma in international relations from the University of the West Indies, and a PhD in international relations from the University of Miami.

Technology is one of the primary connectors of people, places, and possibilities. Most would argue that information and communication technology (ICT) is an indispensable tool in providing connectivity. ICT encompasses all types of "communication technologies such as computers, videos, and the associated hardware, networks and software."[1] On a daily basis, ICT supports, enables, or enhances most of the tasks a fellowships advisor considers essential. Although it is often taken as a given that the growth and pervasiveness of ICT are desirable, researchers are focusing increasingly on both the use of ICT and its effect on and the experience of those employing such tools.[2] Since 1991, when broader World Wide Web access began spreading on college campuses and beyond, potential scholarship and fellowship applicants and their advisors have become more directly connected to these opportunities. What are the consequences of deepening the interdependence between a fellowships advisor's key roles and the ICT used to carry out those tasks? This macrolevel survey reviews core fellowships advisor tasks, assesses basic ICT tools, and discusses their implications for the profession.

Six years ago, NAFA veterans Judy Zang and Paula Goldsmid traded perspectives on what constituted essential advising resources. Of the sixteen commonly used resources Zang referenced, more than one-third were websites or web-based tools, such as the NAFA listserv.[3] Although Goldsmid emphasized human resources—faculty and support staff—she too acknowledged the importance of a "speedy computer, and reasonably good IT help with problems and with new ventures such as setting up a website, and with troubleshooting."[4] While most advising activities still center around direct human interaction, an increasing number of tasks are electronically mediated. By shining a spotlight on the technology-supported ways advisors carry out their mission, I hope in this essay to generate reflection on and further discussion about the changing nature of connectedness in fellowships advising.

How Advisors Use Technology

The list of advisor tasks that benefit from ICT is long. Beyond email and the speedy computer, mobile devices like laptops, tablets, and smartphones are handy tools for remote advising. Dropbox, Microsoft OneDrive, Google Drive, and similar cloud-based file sharing and synchronizing applications can bring the office to the coffeehouse—just in case a student can only meet in the evening after an internship. An informal survey of best practices among several advisors at public and private universities reveals widespread use of software, especially data management programs, web-based applications, specialized services, and organizational tools. In public universities with large enrollments, prospective applicants might be discovered and recruited for discipline-specific awards thanks to institutional student databases like PeopleSoft, GradesFirst, and Banner.

As a starting point, ICT allows advisors to manage student meetings through calendars like Outlook or Access, and advising appointment managers like AdvisorTrac or StarFish. In the case of first- and second-year undergraduates, the advisor may encourage them to document their academic journey and track professional experiences in an electronic portfolio (see Karen Weber's article later in this section). Additionally, advisors can cast a wider net for prospective fellowship applicants by adding an online faculty referral form to their institutional website. More options exist when using other web-based applications, like a premeeting questionnaire that comes directly to an advisor's inbox and generates an automated "thank you" response. This web-based tool opens the door for self-selected applicants to find advisors twenty-four hours a day and makes the time spent getting to know a new advisee more productive. In addition to websites, some of the most popular ICT tools combine productivity and efficiency. Advisors who invite prospective award candidates to an information session using bulk email delivery through MailChimp or Evite can later use those same email addresses to send event evaluations with the help of survey software like SurveyMonkey or Wufoo. Functions that track the number of recipients who open or view messages allow advisors to evaluate the effectiveness of their outreach strategies. Lesser-known programs (Vovici, for example) offer an alternative with a wide range of analytics options.

Some of the most important tools tie valuable methods of point-to-point live video communication, using Skype, FaceTime, Google Hangouts, or GoToMeeting (expect to pay), to the critical task of campus committee evaluations necessary for applicants studying abroad or advisors assisting students preparing for remote interviews. Similarly, access to high-traffic point-multipoint communication tools takes (some) of the stress off advisors who need to make last-minute announcements on Facebook or issue eleventh-hour deadline reminders on Twitter. When it comes to maintaining professional networks and know-how, the NAFA listserv is the go-to source for general querying, historic information, new award and job announcements, collaborative problem solving, and feeling professionally connected.

Finding the Right Technology for the Right Task

Researchers in Pakistan recently proposed three descriptive categories for differentiating among technologies according to their usage outcome.[5] While their proposed model explores the impact of ICT on organizational productivity, the goals in this essay are more limited. Dividing advising tasks based on this system will help tie tasks and tools to outcomes and implications. For the purpose of organization, the multitude of advisor tasks are combined here under five general headings: (1) identifying and evaluating scholarship/fellowship applicants, (2) preparing scholarship applicants, (3) supporting the application and campus collaboration process, (4) promoting scholarship/fellowship awareness, and (5) maintaining professional networks and knowledge. The goal is to indicate the interrelationship between advisor tasks and ICT tools by designating which of the three categories each task aligns with, based on the types of technology used to complete or support the task (see figure 1). These categories, proposed by a group of ICT researchers studying perceived organizational performance in higher education, represent three broad types of technology. The first two categories are "Core Communicational Technology (CCT) including email, Internet search engines and mobile communication; [and] Enterprise Computational Technologies (ECT) including instant messaging software, video conferencing technologies, groupware and online blogs." The final category is Group Collaborative Technologies (GCT) including "knowledge management software, customer relationship management software, project management software, business intelligence and document management solutions."[6]

Figure 1

Advisor tasks	ICT usage categories	Examples of ICT tools
Identify and evaluate scholarship/fellowship applicants	CCT, GCT	email, web-based pre-meeting questionnaire, online faculty referral form, AdvisorTrac, Banner, GradesFirst, PeopleSoft
Prepare scholarship/fellowship applicants	CCT, ECT, GCT	electronic portfolio, search engines, email, Access, Excel, SurveyMonkey, Blackboard, Wufoo
Support application preparation and campus committee evaluation process	CCT, ECT, GCT	electronic transcript delivery service, email, scholarship website, online application systems (Embark), Skype, Google Hangouts, GoToMeeting, FaceTime
Promote scholarship/fellowship awareness	CCT, ECT, GCT	email, electronic newsletter, Facebook, GoToMeeting, Twitter, MailChimp, Evite
Maintain professional network and knowledge	CCT, ECT, GCT	email, scholarship websites, webinars, NAFA listserv, ProFellow, Chronicle.com

The outcome of this basic task analysis shows that a variety of CCT, ECT, and GCT tools are available for almost all five major areas of advisor responsibility. Tasks may require tools from multiple categories, and as is clear from the abbreviated list in figure 1, there are many available tools for each task. Of the three categories, surveyed advisors indicated frequent use of CCT (which includes email) and CGT across all five tasks. Communication technologies are heavily relied on because their primary role is to facilitate rapid, portable, point-to-point or point-multipoint communication appropriate in a higher-education context. Given the prominence of CCT use, more in-depth surveying is required to determine proportionally how much GCT and ECT are utilized. The advisor perspective on whether and to what extent each category of ICT contributes to the successful preparation of national award candidates also deserves further study.

The Implications of Technology Use in Advising

Examining the relationship between fellowships advising and ICT from a task-based perspective certainly gives one an appreciation for the breadth of interaction and possibilities. When viewed, however, from the less tangible perspective of encouraging personal growth and promoting scholarly excellence, a different view emerges. At their core, advisors are constantly counselors and teachers. Some fellowships advisors, especially those enlisted part-time in exchange for a course reduction or stipend, arrive on the job with faculty and teaching experience. A very personalized form of teaching is central to the fellowships advising role. Encouraging students to stretch and grow through the award preparation and application process leads them to discover new possibilities for themselves and their futures. Judith Ramaley, a distinguished scholar and nationally recognized academic leader, recently observed that as technology redefines "the nature and character of discovery," the way we teach "is becoming more about designing the [students'] educational context."[7] While Ramaley's observations focus on scholarly learning, fellowships advisors might ask how the webinars, videos, and electronic portfolios designed to engage students impact the context of their self-discovery. The following potential results of technology use raise more questions worth considering.

One is that ICT may facilitate task efficiency. Advisors who maximize their task efficiency could see increased productivity, better prepared applicants, and, perhaps, more scholarship winners. Although it is beyond the scope of this essay, a follow-up study might investigate the degree to which a correlation exists between effective and efficient use of ICT by advisors and productivity. Likewise an expanded survey weighting use of CCT versus ECT and GCT could add insight into which type of technology adds the most value to a fellowships advisor's role. In recent years, more than one observer has pointed to a narrow focus on winning as the dark side of the scholarship advising process.[8] Indeed, measuring success in such (excruciatingly) narrow terms overlooks the myriad of individual and institutional goals accomplished, regardless of award outcome. Nonetheless, colleges and universities aspire to achieve in all areas. Progress that is defined, however, must be measured; fellowships advising is no exception. When institutions invest deliberately in ICT tools, advisors may experience greater pressure to show returns. A more robust adoption of ICT tools could reduce some kinds of stress (requiring students to review essays using Grammarly or other product prior to requesting a review) while creating others (encouraging a greater dependency on software that can crash or distance the student).

In the advising process, some students self-select for major awards. Others must be sought out and encouraged. Advisors are regularly challenged to find the balance between supporting candidates and grooming them.[9] If ICT skews advisor-student interaction toward efficiency and productivity, will the particular personality traits in ambitious students evidenced by self-selection diminish?

A second possible result that has implications for the advisor is that even strategic use of ICT could have positive and negative impacts on advisees and a fellowships advisors ability to truly support them. Electronic portfolios (shared with an advisor) may provide an efficient tool for regularly monitoring the development of a potentially large number of advisees (such as undergraduates who are Fulbright hopefuls). In a public honors college with enrollment in the hundreds or thousands, this tool may be a time-saver for advisors since fellowships offices rarely enjoy abundant staff. Active and widespread use of the tool by advisees could amplify an advisor's oversight and help refine support strategies. Yet, fewer in-person interactions may cause the advisor to make assumptions about a student's interests and motivations based on the frequency and extent of portfolio updates or based on the information that is shared or is absent. Sparse portfolio entries may give an advisor a limited understanding of the student's potential, so user error should be anticipated. Similarly, heavy reliance on web-based tools that include depersonalized, formulaic prompts, such as "list global experience," may result in a more curated rather than genuine student portrait.

Communication technologies also play a critical role in enhancing the continuity of communication. After an advisor visits an honors seminar to promote scholarships, an electronic message can be delivered to each of the students in the course. ICT allows the advisor to start a conversation. An inquiring student becomes an advisee by responding to the ten-minute prompt and completing an online premeeting questionnaire. Faculty members can also be encouraged to submit easy online student referrals and later become ardent scholarship recommenders to the students they forward to the fellowships office. Through ICT, the core tasks of identifying and evaluating scholarship and fellowship applicants and promoting scholarship and fellowship awareness are significantly enhanced. Advisors can also work with enrollment services to create student listservs as a means to quickly get the message out about scholarship meetings. Email also plays a vital role in the continuity of communication throughout the profession. Fellowships advisors (deliberately and spontaneously) use the NAFA listserv as a forum for digital discourse represented by an email thread.

Finally, if the status quo holds true, an additional result could be that advisors will constantly be confronted with new ICT tools to better perform the same five general tasks. Some will relish the opportunity and challenge of learning a new software or system while others will not. Many advisors may need to devote more professional development time to learning ICT tools, and in smaller offices this may again reduce time with students.

Application Platforms

Clearly, ICT has many implications for the advisor. This is also true for foundations. Applications for major national scholarships and fellowships require online submission of essays, recommendations, transcripts, endorsements, and language evaluations. As recently as 2010, the Rhodes Trust elected its class of scholars for the first time through a fully online process, proving that even the most long-standing traditions are being affected by ICT.[10] But application platforms provide challenges for everyone involved. Former NAFA president Doug Cutchins summarized the challenge well. He observed, "Some of the foundations have their own online applications, and some contract out with third parties. The proprietary applications are often not available for on-campus use, and don't allow for modification for our own usage. Even the best of these proprietary programs have glitches, such as slow speeds during peak periods. Overall, I don't think anyone has yet figured out how to make an online application system that is user-friendly, reliable, cheap, and has full functionality."[11] In this fundamental area of fellowships advising, there are times when the use of ICT causes frustrations for students, advisors, and foundation representatives and begs for a long-term solution.

Using Technology to Expand, Not Replace, Advising

Fellowships advisors have an increasing number of information and communication technology tools intended to enhance communication and collaboration. The tools described are not designed (nor expected), however, to replace the quintessential face-to-face interactions at the heart of fellowships advising. Rather, strategic and thoughtful use of nonessential ICT is important. CCT such as email is essential. As noted, the current level of functionality of some scholarship application platforms is outpaced by advisors' desire for access. The growing pool of scholarship and fellowship applicants poses another ICT challenge. In 2013, the number of U.S. student Fulbright applications topped ten thousand, testing the capacity of Embark in the days before the deadline. Yet, the way fellowships advisors use ICT can improve productivity, enhance effectiveness, lead to better communication, and create new avenues of student support.

Perhaps the most significant impact of ICT on the fellowships advising profession is also its most obvious. It provides greater connectivity. Fellowships advisors are decidedly more available to the students they advise (and in greater numbers), alumni applicants, faculty, the campus community, scholarship sponsors, foundations, and colleagues. In the closing lines of her 2006 list of essential fellowships advising tools, Paula Goldsmid highlighted the importance of "access to communication."[12] Nearly a decade later, her words ring even truer. This general survey of ICT tools available to and used by advisors only hints at the extent to which the profession is being shaped by technology. Ultimately, to be genuinely more connected, advisors must remain aware of the implications of technology use, the professional challenges it presents, and the impact it has on the student throughout the scholarship and fellowship advising experience.

Notes

1. Abbas Zare-ee, "University Teachers' Views on the Use of Information Communication Technologies in Teaching and Research," *TOJET: The Turkish Online Journal of Educational Technology* 10 (2011): 318.

2. See Robert Edmunds, Mary Thorpe, and Grainne Conole, "Student Attitudes toward Use of ICT in Course Work, Work and Social Activity: A Technology Acceptance Model Approach," *British Journal of Educational Technology* 43 (2012): 71–84.

3. Judy Zang, "Resources for Fellowship Advisors," *NAFA Journal,* Summer (2006): 17–19.

4. Paula Goldsmid, "Essential Resources for a Fellowship Advising Office" *NAFA Journal,* Summer (2006): 21.

5. Irfan Saleem, Tahir Qureshi, Saba Mustafa, Farooq Anwar, and Tahir Hijazi, "Role of Information and Communicational Technologies in Perceived Organizational Performance: An Empirical Evidence from Higher Education Sector of Pakistan," *Business Review* 6 (2011): 81–93.

6. Ibid.

7. Judith Ramaley, "How Disruptive Is Information Technology Really?" *Educause Review,* March-April (2013): 8.

8. See Andrew Brownstein, "Ambitious Colleges End the Ivy Lock on Prestigious Fellowships," *Chronicle of Higher Education* 48 (2001): A40–A43; see also Sara Lipka, "Two Victories for a Scholar-Athlete—and Florida State," *Chronicle of Higher Education* 55 (2008): A16–A17.

9. Brownstein, "Ambitious Colleges End the Ivy Lock on Prestigious Fellowships."

10. See www.americanrhodes.org/news-elect.html.

11. Doug Cutchins, email to author, February 2015.

12. Goldsmid, "Essential Resources for a Fellowship Advising Office."

9

ePortfolios and Scholarships Advising

KAREN WEBER

*Karen Weber is the director of the Office of Undergraduate Research at the
University of Houston. In this position, she administers research opportunities,
nationally competitive scholarship initiatives, and the Honors College
ePortfolio program for all undergraduates. Before arriving at the University
of Houston in 2005, Weber worked on nationally competitive scholarships
at the University of Illinois at Chicago. She has been a member of NAFA
since 2003, serving on the Nominations and Elections Committee in 2012
and assisting with print and web materials for the organization. Weber
is currently pursuing a doctoral degree in the College of Education at the
University of Houston; her research focuses on ePortfolios for external
audiences. She was an actress in a previous life, holding a bachelor's degree
from the University of Texas at Arlington, and a master's degree from the
University of Illinois at Chicago in the field.*

have had the privilege of serving as a fellowships advisor for more than a decade, first with students at the University of Illinois at Chicago, and now at the University of Houston. Both of these institutions serve a diverse student population, the University of Houston being the second most ethnically diverse university in the country.[1] Perhaps the most rewarding aspect of this work is watching students grow and prosper as a result of developing their scholarship applications. A beneficial transformation typically occurs during this reflective process; students gain a better understanding of who they are intellectually, professionally, and personally. The number of students who apply each year for these awards, however, is very small. It seemed important and worthwhile to scale the scholarship application process to a larger, more diverse student population so more students would reap the benefits associated with reflecting on past experiences and how those experiences shape their current and future pursuits.

Honors College ePortfolio Program

To address this need, in 2012 the University of Houston's Honors College launched an ePortfolio program for students. The Honors College ePortfolio is a website that showcases students' course work, professional experiences, research, leadership, service, study abroad, and other activities that have shaped their time as an undergraduate. The Honors College is committed to providing students with the curricular and cocurricular experiences they need to be competitive when entering the workforce and graduate and professional school. An ePortfolio is a competency-based tool for students to demonstrate their learning and career readiness to employers, graduate school admissions committees, and even one day perhaps to scholarship foundations.

The ePortfolio development process is twofold. First, at the start of their freshman year during the Honors College Retreat, students are introduced to the ePortfolio program. We encourage students to collect and save the best work from each of their classes. We also ask students to take time to reflect on their academic career each semester and save these reflections with their other archival documents. We ask students to employ "folio thinking . . . a reflective practice that situates and guides the effective use of learning portfolios"—a hallmark of an effective ePortfolio program.[2]

Then, students who choose to share the highlights of their undergraduate career proceed to step two, which is building their ePortfolio to share publicly. Students who wish to "go live" with their site are encouraged to take the one-credit-hour ePortfolio course. The class guides students through the introspective process of building an online profile, a comprehensive self-narrative conveyed through their web pages and artifacts. Our students use Google Sites to build their ePortfolios. We chose Google Sites because it is a free resource, most students are familiar with Google products, it offers a variety of privacy settings, and it provides a wide range of templates and themes that are easy to use. The students also have access to the ePortfolio module we created through Blackboard Learn, the university's online course management system. Through this online folder, students can watch tutorial videos, view sample ePortfolios, and learn how to best develop their particular professional online presence. To model a scholarship application, the module includes questions for students to reflect on such as, "What was your favorite course this year and why? How have you made a difference in your field? Describe your style of leadership." Below are two examples of approaches to constructing an e-Portfolio.

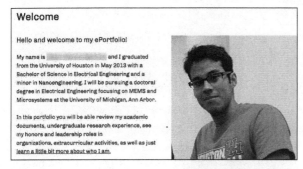

Example 1.

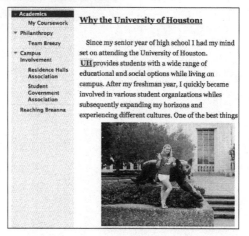

Example 2.

ePortfolio Programs at Diverse Institutions in the United States

The use of ePortfolios continues to expand in higher education because of an increased emphasis on student-centered active learning, an awareness that students enjoy using digital communication technologies, a heightened demand for accountability from colleges and universities, and the knowledge of the current transient nature of workers in the labor force.[3] In developing our particular program, we were interested in the ways in which these other colleges and universities integrated ePortfolio programs within their institutions. Given the importance of ensuring that our ePortfolio program is relevant to the diverse University of Houston student population, we thought it prudent to identify other diverse institutions currently employing ePortfolio programs and to examine how their programs are structured for students.

Among the most well-known ePortfolio initiatives in the United States is the LaGuardia Community College ePortfolio program. Since the program's inception in 2001, thousands of LaGuardia students have created ePortfolios. LaGuardia, located in Long Island City, New York, has partnered with City University of New York (CUNY) colleges Queens and Lehman and with two other community colleges, Queensborough and Bronx, through a five-year Making Transfer Connections Title V grant. The program uses ePortfolios, in addition to other integrative learning practices, to assist students in transferring from community college to a four-year university.[4] This initiative is targeted at creating a supportive infrastructure for Hispanic and low-income students to receive a bachelor's degree.[5] LaGuardia was also awarded a grant through the Fund for the Improvement of Postsecondary Education (FIPSE) program sponsored by the U.S. Department of Education to launch a national ePortfolio research project, which includes participation from twenty-two campuses across the nation.[6] The LaGuardia ePortfolio initiative is an "unusually comprehensive program designed to maximize the development and assessment potential of portfolios."[7]

Lehman College, a partner with LaGuardia in the Making Transfer Connections Title V grant, also supports ePortfolio use.[8] Lehman launched the Pathways to Success, TRiO Student Support Services program in 2010, an initiative funded by the U.S. Department of Education. Oppor-

tunities for students include academic, professional, and personal counseling and programming. Pathways to Success students are encouraged
to develop an ePortfolio throughout their academic career that will become a self-narrative of their life, development, and future aspirations. A
Lehman student's ePortfolio "may include autobiographical statements,
creative works, self-assessments and personal insights, academic records
and milestones, health and wellness information, family history, and
other relevant materials."[9] Clearly the educators at Lehman support students through social pedagogy by connecting their personal background
with their academic experiences to cultivate and enhance student reflection.[10] As a testament to Lehman's success, in partnership with LaGuardia
Community College, Lehman has received several FIPSE grants for developing its ePortfolio programming.[11]

University of Michigan administers a successful "MPortfolio" program. Their program encourages students to use their ePortfolios to make
connections with what they have learned both from life experiences and in
their academic courses, thus "valuing learning from all aspects of life."[12]
For instance, the School of Social Work and the College of Literature,
Science, and the Arts offer a minor titled Community Action and Social
Change, which requires an ePortfolio as the capstone.[13] Students are asked
to reflect on their "personal experiences of transformative civic engagement," which encourages them to identify as agents of social change upon
entering the professional world.[14]

Other diverse institutions, such as Spelman College and Salt Lake
Community College, also require ePortfolios as a component of their academic curricula. Spelman's ePortfolio program—the SpEl.Folio—is part of
the First Year Experience for freshmen, who use it as a tool to document
their learning both within and outside of the classroom. One criterion of
their grading rubric is assessing the "relation of social and academic" within
students' ePortfolios.[15] This encourages students to begin identifying as "social agents, developing their capacity to confront real-world problems."[16]
Salt Lake Community College encourages students to share their ePortfolios with family members, perhaps recognizing the important role familial
support plays in student achievement.[17] Kapi'olani Community College in
Honolulu, Hawaii, whose population comprises primarily Hawaiian students, goes a step further by asking students to use traditional Hawaiian
cultural metaphors within their Learning Experience Assessment Program.[18]

Tidewater Community College, located in Norfolk, Virginia, built an ePortfolio program in support of experiential learning. Tidewater gives portfolio course credit for students who participate in civic engagement, research, and study abroad activities, and then share the experience in their ePortfolios.[19] Students may earn credit hours at any time during their academic careers, which is an important feature of the program, particularly for freshman and sophomore students. It is vital to offer high-impact mentorship programs to students early in their academic careers since these types of experiences may increase retention rates.[20]

Some states have invested heavily in ePortfolio programs. Minnesota has made ePortfolios a statewide initiative for K–16 students and for adults seeking career opportunities through the eFolioMinnesota program, another ePortfolio initiative funded by FIPSE. This free resource for Minnesotans has served more than 250,000 users and has won two national awards for technological advancements.[21] The platform serves as a learning tool for students and as a robust online résumé for job seekers. Although this program is viewed as a success because of how many Minnesotans have taken advantage of the resource, unfortunately no research has been conducted on how eFolioMinnesota might "support learning throughout life."[22]

ePortfolios for Reflection and Identity

ePortfolio use continues to gain momentum throughout the country as a tool for reflection, communication, and assessment. More could be done, however, to reform the current ePortfolio curriculum to encourage students to connect their educational and professional activities with their personal identity. Many students intuitively wish to share information on their origins given the personal nature of an ePortfolio. These pages may be titled "About Me," "More Information," "Coming to the U.S.," or "My History," or, like the example below, "Adapting to the American Culture."

If an instructor guides students through the process of developing their personal narratives and professional experiences and then helps them to connect these elements with other mediums, such as their favorite works of literature and historical or current events, students may progress toward developing a *critical literacy* while developing their ePortfolios. Elizabeth

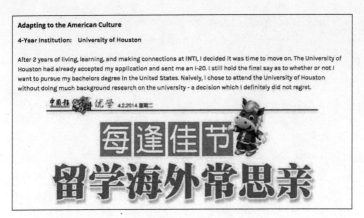

Adapting to the American Culture

4-Year Institution: University of Houston

After 2 years of living, learning, and making connections at INTI, I decided it was time to move on. The University of Houston had already accepted my application and sent me an I-20. I still hold the final say as to whether or not I want to pursue my bachelors degree in the United States. Naively, I chose to attend the University of Houston without doing much background research on the university - a decision which I definitely did not regret.

中国报 优学 4.2.2014 星期二

每逢佳节
留学海外常思亲

Example 3.

Quintero argues that honing critical literacy is essential for urban students to find personal meaning in their studies and may "encourage a natural movement from reflection toward action."[23] Incorporating critical literacy into the curriculum for ePortfolio students is one more way the online platform may be a powerful reflective tool, especially for those students seeking ways to make their education relevant to their personal understanding and experiences. If students feel comfortable sharing information on their background, an ePortfolio has the potential to be a tool for connecting how their cultural background may have shaped or affected their academic and professional path and achievements, and how it may inform their choices and decisions going forward.

Next Steps for ePortfolio

In an effort to more effectively integrate curricular and cocurricular initiatives at the University of Houston, the Honors College is partnering with other units on campus to develop a central clearinghouse of opportunities for all undergraduates. Programs such as ePortfolio, service learning, and undergraduate research would be included in this initiative. If this proposal goes forward, the ePortfolio program would be enhanced and expanded and available to all students at the University of Houston, as well as students enrolled in online degree programs. This comprehensive ePortfolio program will provide students with an eTool to share the highlights of their academic and professional career and demonstrate their transferable skill sets to employers and graduate school admissions committees.

ePortfolios for Scholarships Advising

Although it is unknown if ePortfolios are currently being used by scholarships advisors, this tool could be useful to practitioners in the field. Clearly, applying for major awards hones students' perception of who they are and what they are seeking from their careers, but for those who do not win an award, they may be seeking something more tangible. Encouraging students to develop an ePortfolio before, during, or after they have applied for major awards is an ideal way for them to transfer the reflection process into a tool they can use for other applications, especially when entering the workforce. Developing an ePortfolio before or during the scholarship application process makes students' thought processes and accomplishments more visible to the advisor, and there may be elements on their ePortfolio that candidates did not include in their scholarship application. Candidates' ePortfolios are also helpful in providing information to letter writers supporting students for major awards.

If a potential candidate has an ePortfolio, advisors can use the site as a means of learning more about the student and suggesting awards that may be a good fit. Using ePortfolios is also an easy way to recommend a student for a program or opportunity. For instance, submitting the student's website link to a faculty member who is hiring an undergraduate researcher is much easier than emailing multiple attachments and taking the time to introduce the student. In addition, when promoting a student who has won an award or who has been honored in some fashion, submitting the student's website link is always appreciated by a university's relations or marketing team.

Within a larger framework, the ePortfolio program is a way to scale what we do as advisors for a larger student population. As universities continue to be under scrutiny for how they are preparing students for their next step beyond graduation, educators in higher education must think innovatively about ways for students to better distinguish themselves when attempting to enter the workforce.[24] An ePortfolio program provides evidence of student learning and demonstrates their ability to be competitive in a twenty-first-century workforce. As advisors, we have the opportunity to assist students in developing their online profile and narrative, which can help them achieve their academic and professional goals for years to come.

Notes

1. "Campus Ethnic Diversity, National Universities," *U.S. News and World Report,* 2014, http://colleges.usnews.rankingsandreviews.com/best-colleges/rankings/national-universities/campus-ethnic-diversity.

2. Tracy Light, Helen Chen, and John Ittelson, *Documenting Learning with ePortfolios: A Guide for College Instructors* (San Francisco: Jossey-Bass, 2012), 10.

3. Elizabeth Clark and Bret Eynon, "E-portfolios at 2.0—Surveying the Field," *Peer Review* 11, no. 2 (2009): 18.

4. LaGuardia Community College, "Milestones," 2014, http://www.eportfolio.lagcc.cuny.edu/about/milestones.htm.

5. Ibid.

6. LaGuardia Community College, Fast Facts, 2014, http://www.lagcc.cuny.edu/About/Fast-Facts/.

7. Margarita Benitez and Jessie DeAro, "Realizing Student Success at Hispanic-Serving Institutions," *New Directions for Community Colleges* 204, no. 127 (2004): 43, doi: 10.1002/cc.162.

8. Ibid., 45; LaGuardia Community College, "Milestones."

9. Lehman College, "TRiO Pathways to Success," http://www.lehman.edu/students/trio-pathways-success/.

10. James Hartwick and Richard Mason, "Using Introductory Videos to Enhance ePortfolios and to Make Them Useful in the Hiring Process," *International Journal of ePortfolio* 4, no. 2 (2014): 170.

11. LaGuardia Community College, "Milestones."

12. University of Michigan, "MPortfolio Pedagogy," http://www.mportfolio.umich.edu/pedagogy.html.

13. Katie Richards-Schuster, Mary Ruffolo, Leyda Nicoll, Catherine Distelrath, and Joseph Galura, "Using ePortfolios to Assess Program Goals, Integrative Learning, and Civic Engagement: A Case Example," *International Journal of ePortfolio* 4, no. 2 (2014): 134.

14. Ibid., 136.

15. Spelman College, "FYE Reflection 1 Rubric," http://www.spelman.edu/docs/spelfolio/my-spelman-experience-reflections-rubric.pdf.

16. Jeffrey Duncan-Andrade and Ernest Morrell, *Art of Critical Pedagogy: Possibilities for Moving from Theory to Practice in Urban Schools* (New York: Peter Lang, 2008), 25.

17. Salt Lake City Community College, "General Education," http://www

.slcc.edu/gened/eportfolio/index.aspx; Tim Urdan, Monica Solek, and Erin Schoenfelder, "Students' Perceptions of Family Influences on Their Academic Motivation: A Qualitative Analysis," *European Journal of Psychology of Education* 22, no. 1 (2007): 7–21.

18. Clark and Eynon, "E-portfolios at 2.0," 19.

19. Tidewater Community College, http://www.tcc.edu/central-records/prior-learning-assessments.php.

20. George Kuh, *High-Impact Educational Practices: What They Are, Who Has Access to Them, and Why They Matter* (Washington, DC: Association of American Colleges and Universities, 2008), 9.

21. eFolioMinnesota, "About eFolioMinnesota," http://efoliomn.avenet.net/index.asp?SEC=625D9556-E37C-4837-A0B7-BB27290A7D9A&Type=B_BASIC.

22. Darren Cambridge, "Audience, Integrity, and the Living Document: eFolio Minnesota and Lifelong and Lifewide Learning with ePortfolios," *Computers & Education* 51, no. 3 (2008): 1244, doi:10.1016/j.compedu.2007.11.010.

23. Elizabeth Quintero, "How Can Multiple Literacies Be Used for Literacy Learning in Urban Schools?" in *19 Urban Questions: Teaching in the City*, ed. Shirley R. Steinberg (New York: Peter Lang, 2010), 138–39.

24. Martin Bradley, Robert Seidman, and Steven Painchaud, *Saving Higher Education: The Integrated, Competency-Based Three-Year Bachelor's Degree Program* (San Francisco: Jossey-Bass, 2012), 2.

10

Advanced Placement as a Tool for Scholarship and Fellowship Advisors

SUZANNE MCCRAY

Suzanne McCray, vice provost for enrollment and associate professor of higher education at the University of Arkansas, has also directed the Office of Nationally Competitive Awards since establishing the program in 1998. Prior to assuming the position in enrollment, she was the associate dean of the Honors College. For three years she served on the national program review committee for the Coca-Cola Scholarship, and she currently is on the selection committee for the Morris Udall Scholarship. She has been an active member of NAFA since its founding, serving as its vice president from 2001 to 2003, and its president from 2003 to 2005. She has edited five volumes, including this one of the NAFA proceedings, and was the cochair of the ethics committee that created the NAFA Code of Ethics. Prior to her work at the University of Arkansas, she served as a codirector of the Anglo-American Library at the University of Cluj-Napoca in Cluj, Romania.

onnecting the right student to the right scholarship is a time-consuming and frequently challenging task for fellowships advisors. NAFA conference workshops often focus on this issue. One of the main goals of every advisor is to ensure that students who can be competitive both through the application process and in the academic program of choice understand available opportunities. Field of study, GPA, and faculty recommendations are standard ways of identifying talented students who might be a good match for a particular scholarship.

Searching for students who have taken a significant number of Advanced Placement (AP), International Baccalaureate (IB), or concurrent courses is also an excellent way to find ambitious, academically capable students who often have activity lists that distinguish them from their colleagues.[1] States provide varying levels of opportunities for their students, so not all talented, high-reaching students will have taken AP or IB courses in high school, and identifying students who have taken an ambitious number of such courses is only one additional tool. It certainly should not be used as an exclusive identifier, but it can signal a strong work ethic and intellectual ambition.

Students who reach higher in high school tend to repeat those performances in college. This may be particularly important to public or land grant institutions that serve a broader population of student. Studies indicate that students who perform well on AP and IB exams do not use the hours to graduate early (more on this later). Instead AP and IB credits often allow students time and opportunity (depending on what a given school awards) to take more challenging courses earlier in their college careers, to explore a larger variety of courses, to double major, to spend more time studying abroad and conducting research, to devote additional time to extracurricular activities, and to engage in activities that make them more competitive for national and international scholarships. Even if a school does not grant any credit (most NAFA schools do grant at least some), students who engage in AP and IB work often perform at a high level in college. Those who are now participating in the AP Capstone experience may also have an early start on developing important research skills that could help them engage in research soon after arriving on a college campus.

Advanced Placement and College Performance

National studies indicate that students who take AP (the country's most popular learning acceleration program) in high school and score a three or higher on an exam perform better in college courses and are more likely to graduate. Many of these studies originate with the College Board and may seem suspect, but they are data-driven, peer-reviewed reports and are confirmed by external studies conducted by the Educational Testing Services, the National Center for Postsecondary Research, the National Center for Educational Accountability, and the U.S. Department of Education as well as academic researchers.

Even critics of AP admit that students who participate in AP perform better in college. The questions are usually not about student success but rather about the forces driving that success. Students who take AP and IB classes may simply be more likely to be college-bound students.[2] High schools that have AP courses are likely wealthier, paying more for better teachers, and enrolling students who enjoy smaller classes.[3] Such students are more likely to succeed in any course they take. It may simply be that students who take AP demonstrate in making that choice that they are more motivated and are again more likely to thrive in the academic environment.[4]

A recent and thorough examination of AP and student success, *AP: A Critical Examination of the Advanced Placement Program,* is suspicious of the kudzu-like way AP is continuing to spread. The book contends that students in every high school may not be prepared to do well in rigorous classes, causing them to put in great effort with limited resources that reap little benefit and resulting in some students failing and becoming even less likely to go to college or more likely to do poorly when they arrive there.

Philip Sadler, one of the book's editors, provides key findings at the book's end with advice to (and warnings for) students, parents, teachers, school administrators, college admissions officers, college professors, policy makers, and, finally, the College Board. His description of what students can expect from AP is encouraging: "Advanced Placement courses offer you an opportunity to study a subject in a very rigorous and demanding fashion. You will probably be in a class that has fewer students, those students will likely have stronger backgrounds, and there will be fewer student discipline issues than you have experienced in other courses. Your teacher will have a strong subject matter background and excellent teaching skills."[5] For the ambitious, well-prepared student (and for advisors who later assist them), what's not to like?

Another issue concerns access. Underserved minority students have not always been encouraged to participate in AP courses or when they do, to take the exams. However, the federal government (through subsidies) and many states (through legislation, subsidies, and various college preparation programs) are working to address educational gaps and to provide students from underserved lower socioeconomic groups access to these classes: "The growth of the AP Program in the last decade occurred in part due to increases in federal and state funding, much of which was targeted towards low-income students."[6] According to the Western Interstate Commission for Higher Education (WICHE), thirty-two states have state-level policies related to AP; twelve have policies related to IB.[7] Even critics like Kristin Klopfenstein make clear that the result of federal funding and state support has been a rise in the overall number of participants in AP as well as an increase in the absolute numbers of minority and low-income student participants.

In February 2012, Elizabeth Vardaman, associate dean of Baylor University, and I gave a presentation at the College Board Southwest Regional Forum held in Little Rock, Arkansas, on AP and student success. We provided information on AP as it connected to diversity and to retention and graduation rates at our respective institutions, as well as profiles of students, including those from underrepresented groups, who had both strong AP backgrounds and success in competing for nationally competitive scholarships. It is clear just looking at data for Arkansas and Texas that efforts to improve access are increasing. Arkansas requires at least four core AP classes to be offered in every high school in the state. The state also pays for all AP exams and requires that students take the exam if they want to receive weighted credit for the course. In 2012, the University of Arkansas received 9,770 score reports, an increase of 16.2 percent.[8] The number of Arkansas test takers reporting scores of three or higher increased 10 percent, the number of scores submitted by African Americans increased 13.4 percent, the number reported by Latinos increased 33.5 percent, and the number submitted by low-income students increased by 30 percent.[9]

According to *The 10th Annual AP Report to the Nation* (College Board), African Americans represent 15 percent of the total number of seniors in Texas; 9 percent took an AP exam; and 4.7 percent scored a three or higher.[10] The number is low when compared to Latinos in Texas, who are performing at a higher rate (40.9 percent of seniors are Latino, 41 percent take at least one AP exam, and 35.3 percent score a three or higher [College Board]), but the numbers for all minority groups in Texas are improving.[11]

Texas provides exam fee payments for students with need. More than forty schools in Texas have now implemented the Advanced Placement Incentive Program, which provides cash rewards to both teachers and students for passing scores on AP exams. According to C. Kirabo Jackson, the adoption of the incentive program resulted in improvement not only on the AP exams themselves but also on other nationally normed exams, including the SAT and ACT. What is most encouraging about Jackson's study is this: the greatest positive impact could be found among minority participants.[12] The numbers for underserved groups across the nation are improving; in 2013, 733,416 AP exams were taken by low-income students, and of those, 58.9 percent were minorities.[13] According to researcher Dong Jeong, AP exam subsidies "can serve as an effective policy instrument to reduce socioeconomic disparities in AP exam participation and thereby broaden access to further educational opportunities leading to social equality."[14]

Advanced Placement and Scholarships Advising

THE RECRUITMENT PROCESS

What does this all mean for someone advising students on national and international scholarship applications? Using AP in the recruitment process of potential scholars can be a useful identification tool for the scholarships advisor, allowing a university to identify not only high ability but also early high-achieving students. Most advisors regularly request lists from their institutional research offices of students with high GPAs. Also asking for lists of students who submitted AP scores for consideration either for credit or for admission—or both—can add to the pool of potential scholars. Students who have taken AP, IB, or concurrent enrollment courses in high school are usually ambitious, if not always intellectually curious, students. At institutions where all students selected for admission have strong records of AP, IB, or concurrent enrollment, this list may be less helpful to advisors, but at public, land grant, or regional institutions, the information can be extremely helpful in identifying potential scholars within a large and diverse student body. The level of such engagement (number of courses taken) may be useful information at most schools, pointing to students who embrace challenges, are intellectually curious, and are not simply grade focused.

The push by states to improve successful participation in AP among previously underrepresented groups, including minority students and students with financial need, can mean that a search for students who have taken AP or other rigorous college preparatory courses can also produce names of talented students who may qualify for scholarships that have a need component or that have applications from minorities as a focus. These students, of course, may also be competitive for a wide variety of scholarships.

For the most part, students who get a head start on college in high school are not motivated to do so primarily in order to graduate from college early. Most scholarships advisors know this from their own experiences, and studies confirm that receiving AP credit rarely reduces the amount of time a student spends in college.[15] This may be a criticism of the AP program in general, but from a fellowships advisor's point of view a rush to graduate can limit important, career-shaping experiences. AP credit can allow for a different kind of college experience, one that may include more than one major, additional minors, longer periods of study abroad, extended research efforts, graduate courses, and greater time commitments to service.

In 2013 two million students took approximately 3.6 million exams and sent the results to more than three thousand colleges and universities in the United States.[16] Of the current 429 NAFA institution members, 421 (98 percent) give college credit, exemption, and/or placement of some kind for outstanding performances on AP or IB exams. For advisors at these schools, a search for students who have both performed well on such exams and who have also maintained high GPAs in college is a relatively easy task. For those at universities where credit is not given, a search of scores submitted for admission consideration may prove more difficult, but at the very least a conversation with an applicant about AP/IB/Dual Enrollment could be productive for the letter of institutional endorsement.

LETTERS OF ENDORSEMENT

During the NAFA National General Education UK Symposium held at Cambridge, Gordon Johnson—the conference host and then provost for the Gates Cambridge Scholarship—observed that institutions in the UK were sometimes puzzled by U.S. college transcripts and that the only constant that they felt they confidently understood was the AP credit found on those transcripts.[17] Clearly, programs like AP and IB have a reputation for academic engagement. A student's strong record with such courses can add weight to a transcript, as AP credit is clearly valued by some foundations as a nationally vetted sign of academic preparation and accomplishment.

There are good reasons for this view. Performance on AP exams is a consideration for admission to most top public and private universities and colleges. In an extensive survey of college admissions directors and deans, 91 percent of those interviewed from public institutions and 93 percent from private institutions reported they have policies to include AP performance in consideration for admission.[18] Students who compete successfully for scholarships and who go on to thrive in top graduate programs often have an AP, IB, or concurrent enrollment background. My colleague Elizabeth Vardaman noted in our 2012 presentation that Baylor's recent Fulbright Finalists, for example, earned an average of 15.1 hours of AP credit. Five of the top scholarship recipients at Arkansas in 2013 (Gates Cambridge, Truman, Udall, Goldwater) earned a total of 155 AP hours.[19] Taking AP did not necessarily cause any of these students to be successful in competing for scholarships, but there is a strong correlation, and it points to AP as an excellent tool for identifying competitive students.

Earning a large number of hours through AP or IB can be especially helpful to a student majoring in the sciences. Such a student will be able to begin upper-level courses more quickly and will be able to embrace undergraduate research earlier. These students can have an advantage with scholarships like the Goldwater. Certainly at the University of Arkansas this has proven to be true. Forty of its forty-nine Goldwater Scholars (some attended schools where AP was not offered) together earned approximately 900 total hours of AP credit. This is only a sample of one, but it should encourage campuses that award credit to look at the success rates of their own AP/IB scholars. At our institution, we also keep in mind that nine students did not have any AP or IB credit. Either neither program was offered at their schools, or they were late bloomers. Again, AP searches should be only one among a variety of tools for advisors.

Writers of endorsement letters might want to include a student's AP/IB record in their letters even though the information harkens back to high school. AP and IB credit usually (though not always) appears on the college transcript, and, again, it can be a sign of early academic engagement, helping explain how the student has come to take higher-level courses earlier in the academic career. It can also help less well-known institutions indicate their students are well prepared.

The College Board has now created a new research experience for high school students: the AP College Capstone Program. It was piloted in seventeen schools across the country in fall 2012 and requires a course in the junior year (some take it as early as the sophomore year) that encourages students to conduct research, to review primary sources and secondary sources critically, to develop arguments, to search for solutions, and to "explore real-world issues through a cross-curricular lens and consider multiple points of view to develop a deeper understanding of complex issues."

The student also takes the normal AP courses, and then, in the senior year, the student completes a capstone research project of approximately five thousand words: "Students are evaluated on their ability to design, plan and manage a research project; collect and analyze information; evaluate and make reasoned judgments; and communicate their findings and conclusions."[20] The program developed out of input from higher-education institutions that were concerned the rigor and set curriculum of the AP program might encourage excessive memorization and actually discourage creativity. Fellowships advisors will likely want to watch this program with interest.

Summary

Most scholarships advisors can provide stories of successful candidates (who interviewed for/received the award) for nationally competitive scholarships and fellowships who matriculated with substantial AP or IB credit. Taking AP classes in high school is not a guarantee for retention and graduation from college (though those rates are documentably higher than for non-AP/IB students), much less a guarantee for success in applying for nationally competitive awards. In this essay I do not make a claim for that, address critiques of the program, or promote AP for all.

The argument here is a simple one. Academic rigor embraced early is a good signpost for intellectual preparation and engagement that will serve the student well in college and in graduate programs in the United States and in institutions abroad. Advisors may benefit from using AP and IB course work as an important tool (one of many) in their search for capable students who might be a good fit for a particular scholarship.

A case can also be made for talking with students about their pre-college experiences to see if early preparation may have made a difference in their college programs. Advisors may want to recommend the information be included in letters of endorsement. Students who have been successful in these courses have produced work that has been nationally vetted, and the information may make a transcript more comprehensible to foundations reviewing transcripts from hundreds of institutions. It is true that correlation is not causation, and the strong correlation between AP and student success does not mean that AP is the cause, but for the advisor looking for talented students who could benefit from the scholarship process, correlation is key. Identifying students who have been involved in accelerated learning in high school will likely be productive for the student, the advisor, and even foundations.

Notes

1. The focus of this paper is AP, but IB is an equally challenging program with growing popularity in the United States. AP, IB, or concurrent enrollment can point to ambitious students who are exploring the challenges available to them in their school district.

2. Chrys Dougherty, Lynn Mellor, and Shuling Jian, *The Relationship between Advanced Placement and College Graduation,* 2005 AP Study Series, Report 1 (Austin, TX: National Center for Educational Accountability, 2006), 3.

3. Kristen Klopfenstein and Kathleen Thomas, "The Link between Advanced Placement Experience and Early College Success," *Southern Economic Journal* 75, no. 3 (2009): 874.

4. Dougherty, Mellor, and Jian, *The Relationship between Advanced Placement and College Graduation,* 3.

5. Philip Sadler, "Key Findings," in *AP: A Critical Examination of the Advanced Placement Program,* ed. Philip Sadler, Gerhard Sonnert, Robert Tai, and Kristin Klopfenstein (Cambridge, MA: Harvard Education Press, 2010), 256.

6. Kristin Klopfenstein, "The Advanced Placement Expansion of the 1990s:

How Did Traditionally Underserved Students Fare?" *Education Policy Analysis Archives* 12, no. 68 (2004): 2.

7. Demarée Michelau, "The State Policy Landscape," in *Accelerated Learning Options: Moving the Needle on Access and Success* (Boulder, CO: Western Interstate Commission for Higher Education, 2006), 7.

8. "Summary of AP Scores Reported to University of Arkansas," private report from the College Board to the University of Arkansas, 2012, 3.

9. Ibid.

10. College Board, *The 10th Annual AP Report to the Nation*, 2014, http://apreport.collegeboard.org/.

11. "Advanced Placement Examination Results in Texas and the United States, 2011–2012," Texas Education Agency, Division of Research and Analysis, August 2013: 2–3; retrieved from http://tea.texas.gov/acctres/ap_ib_index.html.

12. See C. Kirabo Jackson, "A Little Now for a Lot Later: A Look at a Texas Advanced Placement Incentive Program," *Journal of Human Resources* 45, no. 3 (2010): 591–639.

13. College Board, *The 10th Annual AP Report to the Nation.*

14. Dong Jeong, "Student Participation and Performance on Advanced Placement Exams: Do State-Sponsored Incentives Make a Difference?" *Education Evaluation and Policy Analysis* 31, no. 4 (2009): 346.

15. Kristin Klopfenstein and M. Kathleen Thomas, "Advanced Placement Participation: Evaluating the Policies of States and Colleges," in *AP: A Critical Examination of the Advanced Placement Program,* ed. Philip Sadler, Gerhard Sonnert, Robert H. Tai, and Kristin Klopfenstein (Boston: Harvard Education Press, 2010), 175.

16. Pam Kerouac, "The College Board Advanced Placement Program," presentation, SEC Enrollment Managers Meeting, Auburn, AL, May 13–15, 2013.

17. Gordon Johnson, comments made at the NAFA Higher Education Symposia in the UK and Ireland, 2006.

18. Colleen Sathre and Cheryl Blanco, "Policies and Practices at Postsecondary Institutions," in *Accelerated Learning Options: Moving the Needle on Access and Success* (Boulder, CO: Western Interstate Commission for Higher Education), 25.

19. See https://lp.collegebaord.org/ap-capstone.

20. Pam Kerouac, "AP Capstone Program and Credential: Program Description, Assessment, and Transcripts," presentation, SEC Enrollment Managers Meeting, Auburn, AL, May 13–15, 2013.

11

How Am I Doing and How Do I Know? Fellowships and Meaningful Assessment

MONIQUE BOURQUE, JULIA GOLDBERG, AND TIM PARSHALL

Monique Bourque is director of Health Professions Advising and Student Fellowships at Willamette University and holds an adjunct appointment in the Environmental and Earth Sciences Department. She received her master's and doctoral degrees in American history and museum studies from the Hagley Fellows program at the University of Delaware. Previously she was fellowships and prizes advisor at Swarthmore College, an assistant dean for postbaccalaureate programs in the College of General Studies at the University of Pennsylvania, and an archivist at several historical libraries in the Philadelphia area. She has served on a range of national scholarship committees. She has published in academic journals including the Journal of the Early Republic, *and in edited collections including NAFA's* All In: Expanding Access through Nationally Competitive Awards *(2013).*

Julia Goldberg is the associate dean of Advising and Co-Curricular Programs responsible for fellowships and health professions programs at Lafayette College, where she has worked since 2002. Prior to that time, she was the director of Scholarships for International Study at the University of Illinois at Urbana-Champaign, and a professor at the University of Wyoming and the University of Nebraska. She holds MAs in history and the teaching of English as an international language from the University of Illinois at Urbana-Champaign, and a PhD in linguistics from Cambridge University. A member of NAFA since its inception, Julia served as coeditor of the NAFA Journal from 2005 to 2007, and as a member of the board of directors from 2009 to 2013. She is the author of "Letters of Endorsement," which appeared in the Journal in July 2006. She serves on various national scholarship selection committees.

Tim Parshall is the director of the Fellowships Office at the University of Missouri-Columbia, a position he has held since 2011. After earning degrees in English from Colgate University and the University of Missouri, Parshall served as a writer and editor and taught part-time. He then spent twenty-five years in higher-education assessment, collaborating with faculty and administrators at the University of Missouri and at colleges and universities across the country, helping them to establish clear goals, to devise strategies for achieving those goals, and to analyze and improve implementation efforts. His assessment experience includes work in both academic and student affairs and is predicated on what he calls "a covenant of quality," through which people with a common purpose form a bond and work together to achieve agreed-upon goals.

As colleges and universities grapple with how best to position themselves within the shifting educational environment and struggle with a range of budgetary issues and stakeholder concerns, fellowships programs are increasingly asked to justify their existence and worth to the overall mission of the institution itself. Planning an office review or assessment to address these concerns can be a daunting process, requiring a substantial commitment of time and cooperation from a range of offices across campus. In 2007, Meg Franklin published a seminal report in the *NAFA Journal* on how to undertake the assessment of a fellowships office.[1] Our purpose is not to do so again but to offer our insights and perspectives and to raise questions about what can or should be assessed. Our comments reflect our differing degrees of familiarity with the formal assessment process, ranging from someone new to the process, to one who has served as an assessment professional prior to becoming a fellowships advisor, to one who has served as an external evaluator. Yet we share remarkably similar views and advice regarding the need to thoroughly and meaningfully situate the fellowships office within the larger institutional context prior to embarking upon the formulation of an assessment plan and the collection of data. This essay provides a discussion of issues that might be considered and offers an example of how the assessment process might best proceed, resulting in a useful collection of evidence and an interpretation and discussion of the findings.

One of the lessons learned at a 2012 NAFA summer workshop on "A Holistic Approach to Fellowship Advising," and at the seventh biennial NAFA conference in 2013 on "Focusing on the Scholar in the Scholarship Process," is that many advisors are facing similar sorts of assessment challenges. NAFA has a strategic role to play in guiding assessments as a repository of models, rubrics, and metrics and as a resource for collegial advice and a forum for debate. The newly constituted NAFA committee on assessment is a step in the right direction, particularly if the committee provides guidance and support while developing an initial set of "best practices." The profession also needs assessment criteria, trained mentors, and external evaluators. Resources, models, and protocols adaptable to different institutional needs and practices are also critically important. Sharing tools, insights, concerns, successes, strategies, and models will help us all be more strategic and reflective, less harried and uncertain, and more valuable to our institutions and to the students we advise.

The Value of Assessment

Although it can be intimidating, particularly for those facing a formal review for the first time, framing an assessment plan can be a valuable opportunity to better understand and locate the fellowships office's role within the institution. This larger framework will be essential for situating an office's work vis-à-vis the institution's mission and goals as well as providing the context needed to interpret or evaluate what *should* be measured and what are reasonable future goals and practical next steps.

The prospect of a formalized office assessment is one that many advisors face. Some do it, some avoid it, some welcome it, and others fear it. Nevertheless, most do it, whether formally, semiformally, or very informally. Advisors (and foundations) engage in assessment for annual reports, during performance reviews, for personal satisfaction, or out of curiosity. And all too often, we do it without even *thinking* about what we are doing. If approached correctly, assessment can be both rewarding and revelatory, allowing advisors to adjust their sights, better attain the institution's vision and goals, and improve services. However, if done "incorrectly" or without adequate regard to what kinds of information an awards office truly needs to know, assessment can become "the monster under the bed," sending advisors down avenues of data collection that *seem* meaningless or unhelpful, chewing up valuable resources (time, energy, personnel, etc.) when most advisors are already stretched to the limit, juggling a calendar full of campus and official deadlines, information meetings, and everything in between. These pressures become even more intense if the fellowships program is but one of multiple duties performed by the office director.

Assessment: What Is It?

Briefly, the assessment process is intended to iteratively and systematically report and reflect upon how well an office meets its stated goals. The problem is distilling the essence of *what* to collect, *how* to interpret the findings, *why* use a particular reporting method, and *who* needs to know the results. Do the office's assessment goals coincide with the administration's interest in what we do? What are we setting out to accomplish? Why? Are we actually accomplishing it? How do we know? Are we satisfied with the outcomes? What can we do to improve?

Assessment models abound (see figure 1 for an example). Most situate the process and the data collection employed within the larger context of the institution and the office's location within the organization. This contextualization is important. Yet all too often the assessment procedures

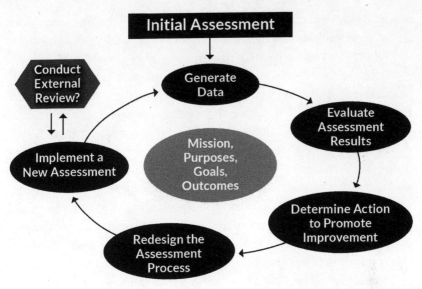

Figure 1.

in which we engage, as well as the criteria driving that assessment, are adopted without critical forethought. Failing to spend time at the outset situating the office within the larger institutional context can have significant ramifications for what we assess, how we interpret the information gathered, how we improve our services, and what we contribute to the overall goals of our institution.

Context: What Should Be Considered?

Offices charged with advising students about competitive awards should fit squarely within the institution's mission, strategic plan, organizational structure, and faculty culture. Additionally, advisors should consider the rationale for the program's existence and the advisor's job description. Thoroughly considering overarching facets of the office should be the first step and should reflect the mission statement and operational and program goals. These factors play directly into how to frame meaningful questions and will provide the means to better interpret the data collected, leading to a greater likelihood of real improvement as a result. Failing to take the time to contextualize the office—to address goals, mission, staff size, processes, space, reporting structures, and assessment needs—inevitably results in the adoption of ill-fitting or meaningless assessment criteria and evidential measures.

All too often the assessment advisors engage in, as well as the criteria driving that assessment, is adopted without critical forethought. Fellowships offices are particularly prone to adopting ill-fitting models, largely because the office's very reason for existence tends to vary. Trying to find the single assessment model that fits all is just not possible because of the variety of environmental contexts for these offices. In some cases the fellowships office is considered a service provided by student affairs, often an outgrowth of career services. At other institutions the program may be perceived as integral to the intellectual development of the student and is housed in academic affairs. For some institutions, although this is rare, it may be part of an enrollment services unit.

In addition to location, there is also the question of the nature of the work advisors do with students and the validity of the statistical measures that advisors may employ. The population of potential applicants is a tiny fraction of the student body, and contact hours with any individual student are relatively few compared with the hours a student will spend working with faculty in a single class. Fellowships advisors see students at different stages in students' careers; some may work only with programs that require the advisor to be the gatekeeper to applications that require nominations. In all cases, the advisor is the bearer of disappointing or exciting news, the one who asks the difficult questions, demanding hours of time in application preparation for a limited number of students. What constitutes success or failure in this context?

The Work That We Do

Fellowships offices exist to facilitate and pave the way for application submissions. The key here is *facilitate*. For some, the home institution allows staffing only for part-time advising programs and provides minimal support and resource allocations under the assumption that all that is really required of such an office is to distribute information to students about opportunities and to ensure applications are being completed and submitted in a timely manner. The office or program may have been conceived simply as the repository and distributor of information to relevant constituents (e.g., students in certain majors, those with financial need, those with particular GPAs, etc.). Many advisors' job descriptions reflect this assumption. Most advisors are asked to manage an office, to have strong organizational and communication skills, and to be the keepers of the evidence—counting the number of inquiries, student contact hours, applicants, and positive outcomes. For assessment purposes, it is important to know how well the advisor got the word out, what methods were employed to inform students, and what more could or should be done.

Over time, that initial intention and rationale for maintaining a fellowships office have morphed along the lines of *paving* the way for the submission of competitive applicants by *developing* scholars. Their successes have become a measure of an individual institution's strength, reflecting the quality of the student body nurtured at the hands of stellar faculty through excellent academic programs and by dint of the extra-curricular and cocurricular opportunities and resources offered. With that slight shift comes the burden of proof—a burden that the fellowships office is asked to provide. This shifts the assessment of students' engagement toward counting honorable mentions, finalists, and winners and then comparing how that institution's applicants fared against peer institutions. Once we tacitly accept this shift in job responsibility, the assessment criteria and measures will follow suit.

Recognizing that the chances of winning fellowships are quite small (in some cases as low as 2 percent), fellowships programs tout the benefits of applying—benefits such as applicants becoming better writers or speakers, developing a clearer sense of values, giving voice to a vision and career aspirations, and so on. In the current educational landscape these benefits are considered "learning outcomes," and as such, they are subject to assessment.

How do advisors measure these learning outcomes? Are those measures statistically meaningful? Here it is important to consider the students themselves and the way fellowships advisors work with them. Advisors work with high-achieving students for a short period of time. Is it reasonable to expect significant improvement in writing clarity between draft one and draft five, and were we hired to teach critical thinking or communication skills? If so, how do we define success, and does this loop us back to whether or not the student won?

When considering the assessment process, keep in mind that advising offices are but a small cog in the student's overall development. Mission statements must reflect the advisor's role in the process. It is important not to lay claims to learning outcomes that cannot be readily assessed, nor to ones for which the advisor does not want to be held accountable. Again, consider the job description. Was the fellowships advisor hired to be a writing or public speaking tutor? Did the job description include teaching critical thinking skills or serving as a career counselor or academic advisor? Some of this may be overtly stated in job descriptions, although this is likely rare, and sometimes it may simply be implied in "assisting students."

When collecting data, keep in mind that the numbers are small, advising services are often limited to one or two meetings, and successes can be difficult to measure. If improperly constituted, the metrics selected and data gathered will fail to generate the understanding we seek. For an office that is designed to provide information, track applications, select appropriate nominees, and count the winners, assessments will likely include the following:

- the number of students advised
- an honorable mention, alternate, finalist, and scholar count
- comparisons to benchmark institutions
- alternative winning (success with graduate, law, and medical school applications and even awards from those institutions)
- faculty mentors involved in the process
- number of departments working collaboratively with the office
- total dollar amount of funding students received

Office Location

Consider where the office is located within the institution (see figure 2). Is it located within student or academic affairs? When considering location, questions an advisor may want to may ask while developing an assessment plan include the following:

- How well integrated is the advising office within the overarching student development framework?
- Is the office a shop where students typically visit only once or twice,

or is the office a well-integrated, essential cog in the student development flow chart?

- How do students find their way to the office?
- Do faculty and others regularly refer students?
- How can the situation be improved?
- In what other ways do faculty, departments, and other campus programs promote the work being done in the office?

Finally, consider the cohort institutions against which advisors may be asked to measure success. When comparing scholarship outcomes (winners and honorable mentions) against benchmark schools, first make sure those schools bear comparison. The list of institutions from the provost's or president's office may differ from those provided by the admissions office. Find out the intention behind the list provided: Is it a list intended for comparing faculty salaries or benefits, or does it represent institutions with similar student profiles? Then consider the strengths and cultures of those cohort institutions. For example, if the institution does not have a strong STEM program, it might not be productive to compare the work of the scholarships advising office to institutions with exceptionally strong STEM programs. Similarly, if the advising office is at an

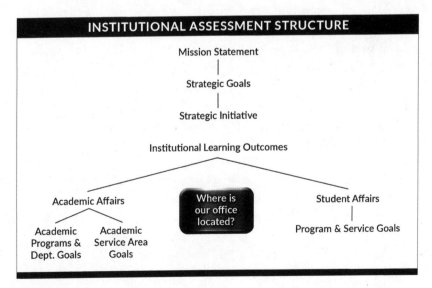

Figure 2.

institution with a strong creative arts program, it is probably not useful to make comparisons to institutions that have weaker creative arts programs. That said, if advisors find that the institution is "slipping" compared to what the administration had previously considered to be weaker schools within the cohort list, it is important to include this in an assessment. It may prove beneficial to find out what it is that benchmark schools are doing that consistently leads to their successful showing with individual scholarships, especially if they seem to be punching above the weights of their institutional programs.

Viewed in this way, if done correctly, assessment can be useful for the institution and for scholarships advisors because it can illuminate areas where the program is effectively providing assistance to students and building successful institution-wide partnerships on the one hand, and can point to areas for further growth and collaboration on the other. An effective assessment can reveal some "hard truths" about the type of student the institution attracts through its admissions policies, and how well the fellowships advising office holistically and strategically engages in student development. A campus culture that promotes student research, civic engagement, and integrated learning opportunities is one that develops many of the basic characteristics we seek in our applicants. However, advising offices cannot establish this culture alone. Ultimately, admissions, the registrar's office, faculty, and career services (especially convenient for those advising offices housed in career services) are our natural partners in the process of attracting and working with students. In the absence of such strong partnerships, the fellowships office may be left to do most of the "heavy lifting"—creating a culture where students actively seek our office, act on the opportunities advertised, and do so without the active encouragement and support of their academic and cocurricular mentors.

If assessment is about understanding who we are and what we do well, or not so well, we should ask ourselves tough questions about the quality and type of students the institution attracts, and what happens to those students after they arrive on campus:

- Who does the institution admit as first-years?
- Who does the institution support with four-year merit scholarships? What are the institution's expectations of those merit scholars?

- Who are the students admitted into the honors colleges or programs (if such programs exist at the institution)?
- What programming, messages, expectations, and challenges does
  the institution set before exceptional students?
- Does the institution assume that its merit scholars will constitute
  the bulk of fellowship applicants and recipients? Do the data support such assumptions?
- Does the institution attract and admit self-starters, outside-the-box
  thinkers, visionaries, and social entrepreneurs? How are such students
  doing in the fellowship application process? Are they applying?
  Do they outpace the merit scholars when it comes to fellowship
  outcomes? Why?

Asking these questions will also provide a context for assessing the
scholarships office work as well as that of the institution itself. It will indicate the caliber of students, the demographic area (regional, major, etc.)
from which they tend to be selected, and whether or not the results of
the competitions match what could be expected of the student body. It
might also point to institutional issues and office challenges. There may
be a need to reevaluate the criteria employed in selecting merit scholars as
well as the selection criteria employed by fellowship committees. When
interpreting the data, keep in mind that the fellowships office cannot create competitive students, nor can it develop their scholarship potential. At
the onset, potentially competitive students must attend the institution if a
campus "talent identification program," which advisors may be expected
to develop and populate, is going to be successful.

Selecting Assessment Criteria and Metrics

While as advisors we must find ways to provide assessments of our work,
we must avoid falling into the trap of employing metrics and gathering
data that are easily obtained but that reductively (de)limit what others
might mistakenly uphold as evidence of that work. That said, there are
instances in which counting makes sense and can contribute meaningfully to articulating and unpacking how successful we have been in working toward office goals. If, for example, we are charged with informing
students about opportunities, it is easy to simply count the number of

classes visited, presentations given, or student office appointments held. But are these data, by themselves, meaningful? Is collecting such data a worthwhile use of our time?

Each year we should certainly document both consistency and growth in our program by reporting the numbers of applicants per fellowship and the numbers of finalists and recipients. But we need to place those bits of information in context. The data must serve a broader and deeper purpose. Thus, for example, *how many* students we have spoken to in a given year might not mean much, but *which ones* we met with could be significant. While we may easily be able to ratchet up numbers by visiting large enrollment courses, the "yield" may ultimately be lower than visiting those smaller, niche classes where the likelihood of instilling student interest is higher. In the assessment review it is imperative that we contextualize the data and provide a rationale for our activities to guard against unrealistic expectations.

In addition to reporting how many students applied for specific fellowship programs, we should use those numbers as the point of entry to asking the more insightful questions about why individual students applied, while others did not. Did we target the appropriate group of students? Do the numbers have anything to do with faculty encouragement or support? Do we need to redouble our efforts to ensure that students are made aware of the opportunity? Are we inadvertently excluding students? Do we need to improve our outreach to faculty? And what of the students? Do they opt not to apply because the monetary value of the award is small (a mere drop in the tuition-and-fees bucket at many private colleges) and the likelihood of winning is even smaller? How do we educate students, parents, and faculty about the intrinsic and extrinsic value of applying?

For years one advisor put out a targeted call for Goldwater applicants that went to sophomores at the start of the fall semester who had already declared their major. After analyzing who was targeted, the advisor realized that students who had not yet declared a major were inadvertently being excluded. Another advisor realized after analyzing the data that the university's mathematics department rarely nominated or encouraged students to apply for the Goldwater. This situation was exacerbated by the nature of the "call for applicants" and information materials that touted the importance of engagement in research. Math majors often do not engage in research until their junior or senior year, and so faculty assumed they could not put forward a competitive application. For all of these rea-sons, it was the rare math major that would submit a campus application. Once it became clear that math students can demonstrate competitiveness based on their participation in math competitions, such as the Putnam Exam, or on future research interests, the number of math students that applied to the Goldwater increased. Advising offices at institutions with strong math departments will want to make sure their Goldwater materi-als include these kinds of options. To tease out these kinds of issues, a careful assessment of who is responding to flyers, emails, and other office materials and which departments are nominating students is critical.

A Word about Surveys

Maintain a healthy skepticism of surveys and questionnaires, particularly those designed to assess student satisfaction with services rendered. While some critics do not care for what they see as the softness of self-reported data, significant concerns arise also from a combination of the popula-tion surveyed and the rates of return, which are often rather low and can be distorted by extreme responses. Students attend onetime events, such as information sessions, for so many different reasons that it is difficult to trust the validity of the responses provided. Advisors should also be mindful that the responses of those engaged in the application process may be akin to those provided on course or teacher evaluations—little more than a reflection of the student's (dis)pleasure with the advisor's re-action to the most recent draft or the outcomes of the competition.

What may be more helpful than satisfaction surveys handed out after each session or individual meeting is obtaining evidence of the long-term impact of the advising work. A more effective approach might be to em-ploy questionnaires sent out in the context of analyzing the overall under-graduate experience and the student's awareness of the office's existence. These questionnaires could include questions about when and how often the student met with the fellowships advisor, why students did or did not avail themselves of the services provided, and others designed to "get at" the roles that the fellowships office and the application process played in students' personal and professional development. This is where assessment instruments like the National Survey of Student Engagement (NSSE) may become useful, particularly if the institution is able to include some of its own questions that are designed to understand and place the fellowships advising office within the framework of student development and institution culture.

Collaborating with alumni offices and institutional research staff can also be helpful, allowing fellowships offices to connect with students with whom they have worked most closely, because these students may have the best understanding (or the most pointed criticism) of the utility of going through the process—those learning outcomes we promote as the value that accrues from spending a great deal of energy writing, rewriting, discussing, and contemplating personal values and career goals.

Learning Outcomes

Increasingly, our offices are asked to assess the learning outcomes for students who go through the application process. This sounds reasonable; after all, it is an argument that is made to justify our office's existence and role within the institution's mission, not to mention one that NAFA extols (e.g., the 2003 conference "Beyond Winning: National Scholarship Competitions and the Student Experience"). Fellowships advisors maintain that there is "value added" for students going through an application process. This added value includes claims that students will become better writers or communicators, better able to draw connections between their otherwise seemingly discrete experiences (courses, research papers, internships, extracurricular activities, etc.), and better able to understand themselves and their educational, intellectual, and career trajectories. Having made such claims, advisors can be expected to prove them. This is where the question of learning outcomes becomes problematic on a number of levels. To begin with, learning outcomes are formulated as measurable rubrics with the burden of proof falling more upon the "imparter" of the learning than the learner. If advisors are hired to do any of the above, or if we specifically make claims about accomplishing any of the above, then the question of learning outcomes is relevant and one that we should reasonably be expected to address. Nevertheless, scholarships advisors need to be very careful in how we assess and report such learning outcomes.

Take, for example, the relatively easy learning outcome of improved writing. Of course advisors should expect to see an improvement between the first and final draft of the essays that are submitted to us. But has the student really learned to be a better writer? It seems likely that an advisor will not know if students have become better writers until the next time they apply for a fellowship and submit an application essay, and with some students that may never happen. If students should submit another application, would it really be possible to claim those who provided better written applications benefited from the previous interactions with the office? Even should such writing improvements occur, it will difficult to measure or to claim the improvements are the result of prior work with the advisor.

Now take the question of whether students acquire a better understanding of their goals or values. This is an even trickier learning outcome to assess. An advisor can employ a rubric for assessing improvement between written drafts, but how can one measure the student's sense of personal growth without reliance upon self-reporting and anecdotal evidence? Surveys can be used, but questions of when and how often to administer them arise, not to mention that the confidence in such a survey can be problematic. Subject numbers are so small that a response in one direction or another on even a five-point Likert scale from one respondent can swing results in widely differing directions. What about internal versus external locus of control factors? What about students who are disappointed in not being selected by the campus committee as opposed to those who are endorsed? Timing, too, is important: often students do not report having experienced growth until months or years later.

The likelihood of being asked to assess learning outcomes increases if the fellowships office is located under academic affairs or if the office includes reference to learning outcomes in its mission statement, strategic plans, or services rendered statement. Consider, for example, the following two mission statements:

1. The fellowships office advises and prepares students to compete for national fellowships and awards. From the initial inquiry to the nomination and selection stages, the office works with current students and recent graduates as they prepare competitive applications. As a consequence of the reflection and challenge involved in the application process, students will discover the means of enhancing their educational experiences while learning how to define their goals and acquire the necessary skills to achieve them.

2. The mission of the fellowships office is to (a) educate and inform, (b) support, and (c) develop applicants through the process of applying for prestigious awards.

The first statement makes reference to learning outcomes (defining goals, acquiring skills); the second does not. This may simply be because the second statement is sufficiently vague.

Internal and External Evaluators

Advisors faced with a full-fledged review replete with internal and external evaluators should think carefully about which entities on and off campus to involve and how the process can be structured so as to involve all parties in substantive discussion about mission and goals as well as measurable results. When considering administrative units and the individuals to participate in the review, advisors need to carefully identify and bring in the most appropriate administrative and faculty partners from across the institution. These partners may not be those who connect most frequently with the fellowships office (e.g., the registrar, the honors college, and career services). Instead, advisors may choose to include those individuals and offices or programs that have collaborated with the scholarships office in serving students, including writing centers, civic engagement programs, and research groups.

In these days of tightening resources, it might be important to solidify an office's position independent of the numbers of scholarship and fellowship awards, drawing attention to collaborative or creative programming efforts that cross campus boundaries. Moreover, in most cases these units or individual faculty members are able to provide the most useful feedback about what we are doing and how well we are doing it. They are the ones who can best articulate how their work connects to the institution's or the administrative division's strategic plan. These colleagues will be the ones who have spent time thinking about how the awards office's work complemented their own and the effectiveness of those collaborative efforts. These should be individuals who have joined the advisor in thinking about office functions that can work cooperatively, resulting in information exchanges or routinely referred students. Explaining these collaborations in annual and administrative reports will also be an opportunity for advisors to connect to senior administrators who may not be very familiar with their offices.

The assessment process should also include an informed external perspective. Whenever possible, advisors should bring in more than one external reviewer; including at least one peer and one aspirational institution would be ideal. A diversity of perspectives is important. While a representative from a college or university much like one's own can better evaluate and understand the work done and challenges faced, a representative from a very different institution can provide useful, fresh insights and ideas regarding how to handle administrative or programming concerns or other issues. Finally, by also bringing in multiple groups from across campus in addition to external reviewers, we can help to minimize the danger of inadvertently assessing the person in charge of the office rather than the office itself.

Assessment 101

Before embarking on an office or program assessment, advisors should re-read the mission statement. Does it need revision? If so, this should be part of the assessment planning process, which will be most successful if it is undertaken with the institution's goals and strategic plan in mind. Being aware of these charges can help advisors realistically think through what to assess and why. If the assessment is formal, one done as part of an institution-wide review, it is important for advisors to meet with the appropriate administrative entities and establish the ground rules for the process. Without understanding the larger context for review, advisors may feel disconnected, engaging in a process that feels wrong and asking the "wrong" questions. Fellowships advisors need to also ensure that they examine from different angles the questions that are driving the assessment. Advisors do not have to assess everything. In fact, it might be better to use one or two fellowships programs as a measuring stick (e.g., Goldwater and Fulbright) rather than all fellowships or all office functions.

An Example of Assessment Planning

As advisors enter the early stages of assessment planning or are facing the need to do so, they may find useful a tool one advisor has found helpful in mapping the initial stages of an assessment process and creating a structure for undertaking regular assessment at his institution. What follows is a portion of the assessment plan Tim Parshall prepared for the Fellowships Office at the University of Missouri-Columbia (MU) late in the 2011–12 academic year, toward the end of his initial year as the first full-time professional in the office. At that time, Parshall believed it important not only to establish goals and plans of action but also to explain the rationale for the structure of the document, as most of those reading the report were not familiar with the format that MU was putting in place for academic assessment and planning. Therefore, he treats the assessment plan as a living document whose primary purpose is to make clear the office's aspirational goals and to outline strategies for achieving those goals. Since presenting the original document to his vice provost, Parshall has updated the vice provost and his advisory committee at least once a year on what has proven to be effective and, to the extent possible, why it is working. Parshall found that it is incumbent upon him, as the director of the Fellowships Office, to provide evidence not just through the numbers (how many finalists and how many office visits, for example) but, more importantly, through the "learning outcomes" and the office partnerships that demonstrate that students, faculty, and staff are getting more involved in the processes that his office manages. Because the number of applicants for any given fellowship may be quite small, he relies, of necessity, on anecdotal evidence—direct feedback from students and faculty on the utility and effectiveness of what he does. He also looks for evidence of student growth, whether improvement from one iteration of an application essay to another or self-reports of personal development, and pays attention to increasingly higher rates of faculty willing to share reference letters for review (not censorship) with the Fellowships Office and/or with other recommenders for the same student.

Mission Statement

The fundamental purpose of the (MU) Fellowships Office is to identify high-ability and high-achieving students as early as possible in their academic careers and to assist them in developing their potential as candidates for nationally competitive fellowships. While only some of our applicants will be selected for these awards, all should gain insight into themselves—their skills, their aspirations, and their prospects for future achievement. Student development stands at the forefront of our mission, and we strive to assist students as they come to grow into the university's four core values: Discovery, Excellence, Respect, and Responsibility.

Aspirational Goals

1. A systematic program to assist high-ability, high-achieving students learn about fellowship opportunities and take advantage of services provided by the Fellowships Office.
2. Knowledgeable full- and part-time staff, augmented by supportive faculty, who provide necessary training and resources to the students and faculty who use Fellowships Office services.
3. Applicants for scholarships and fellowships who are well prepared to compete with students from across the nation for prestigious awards.
4. Faculty and staff who have knowledge of fellowship opportunities for their students, know about services provided by the Fellowships Office, and collaborate with the Fellowships Office in assisting students with the application process for competitive awards.

So how do the four goals of the MU Fellowships Office play out in connection to assessment?

- First, the **goals** remain more or less fixed.
- Next, the office established broad **strategies** for achieving the goals; the strategies should be stable, with little change from year to year, although we pay attention to see how well these parts of the overall plan are working.
- The particular **tactics** the MU office employs—specific methods by which we put strategies into practice—might shift even from one month or event to the next. (For example, one summer, during orientation sessions for incoming first-years, the director observed that one promotional piece attracted more attention than another; therefore, he altered his tactics by giving greater prominence to that attention getter than to others.)

Below is the opening section of an assessment of Goal 3, with some general remarks for the benefit of the MU advising committee, as well as for the vice provost, followed just by the first strategy and some commentary.

3. Applicants for scholarships and fellowships who are well prepared to compete with students from across the nation for prestigious awards.

During information sessions, we emphasize two main points: Students need to begin building portfolios early in their college careers; faculty and staff in a position to identify likely candidates for fellowships should urge those students to meet with Fellowships Office staff and/or contact us about those students—again, the earlier the better. In addition, we strongly encourage students to identify faculty (and others) whom they can cultivate as potential mentors and writers of recommendation letters (those relationships cannot be stressed enough).

The strategies that follow intertwine and are linked inextricably with the elements of Goal 4 that get at knowledgeable faculty and staff around campus: The more all of us know, the more that all of us pay attention, the more successful this office will be in promoting fellowships opportunities and in increasing the number of qualified students who prepare strong applications for those fellowships.

- Identify potential candidates through various campus sources (e.g., registrar, academic advisors, student affairs professionals, faculty members, others who lead programs that supplement student services in academic affairs).
- In meeting with individuals and groups across campus, we continue to try to learn (and implement) the approaches that those people believe will be most effective *in their programs*. While we are paying special attention to early identification, we are also striving to contact individuals and programs with the best fit for particular fellowships.
- It is relatively easy to target students in STEM fields for Goldwater or in environmental fields for Udall, and we can place heavy emphasis on students in Arabic, Chinese, Japanese, Korean, and

Russian classes (among others) for Critical Language and Boren scholarships. Similarly, we can focus on faculty and students in the sciences, engineering, and the social sciences for NSF Graduate Research Fellowships. With Fulbright, we have made headway in scientific and agricultural fields through the direct assistance of the director of Fulbright's U.S. Student Programs visit to campus.

- Yet some areas are simply more difficult to access in part because students in those fields *tend* to have chosen those majors as direct preparation for careers (e.g., teacher preparation and business) or because the focus of the field tends toward one-on-one clinical work (e.g., nursing, social work, and many of the majors in Human Environmental Sciences and the School of Health Professions).

Conclusion

In this essay, we have discussed how the context drives the measures, how the data must be situated in order to be meaningfully interpreted, and the importance of asking difficult questions as a means for improving our services and outcomes. We contend that in the absence of locating the fellowships office within the larger institutional context, it is easy to adopt assessment measures and report data that may be less than revelatory for the continued growth of our office and institution. While we have not operationalized the assessment process, we have stressed the importance of asking questions that will help advisors make sense of the data collected and contribute to the framing of operational goals and strategic plans.

For assessment to be meaningful, it must be able to illuminate areas where the office is strong, where it needs work, and where it can provide assistance or play an integral role in the institution's mission and strategic plan. Such an assessment can also indicate areas where advisors can form institution-wide partnerships, contributing to areas for further growth and collaboration. A fellowships office assessment can also reveal some hard truths about the demographics of the student body and how the institution holistically and strategically engages in student development. Establishing a campus culture that promotes student research, civic engagement, and integrated learning opportunities is likewise important in developing many of the basic characteristics sought in applicants. Ultimately, admissions, faculty, and career services, as well as honors programs (where available), are or must become our natural partners in the process of attracting and working with students. In the end, the assessment should serve to validate and remind the administration, trustees, and other stakeholders of the value of the office and the myriad ways the office and advisor's work contributes to the institution's mission and educational values.

Note

1. Meg Franklin, "Assessment of Fellowship Programs," *NAFA Journal*, Summer 2007, 22–27.

Appendix A

THE NATIONAL ASSOCIATION OF FELLOWSHIPS ADVISORS EXECUTIVE BOARD

Joanne Brzinski, President	Emory University
Dana Kuchem, Vice President	Ohio State University
David Schug, Treasurer	University of Illinois at Urbana-Champaign
Alicia Hayes, Secretary	University of California, Berkeley
Laura Damuth, Board Member	University of Nebraska-Lincoln
Belinda Redden, Board Member	University of Rochester
Lyn Fulton, Board Member	Vanderbilt University
Jill Deans, Board Member	University of Connecticut
Robin Chang, Board Member	University of Washington
Tony Cashman, Board Member	University of Holy Cross
Stephanie Wallach, Board Member	Carnegie Mellon University
Robyn Curtis, Board Member	University of Southern Mississippi
Kyle Mox, Board Member	University of Chicago
Brian Souder, Board Member	University of Maryland Baltimore County
Tara Yglesias, Foundation Representative	Truman Scholarship Foundation
Sue Sharp, Foundation Representative	IIE/Boren
Lisa Kooperman, Communications Director	Vassar College

FOUNDATION MEMBERS OF THE NATIONAL ASSOCIATION OF FELLOWSHIPS ADVISORS

American Councils for International Education

American Society For Engineering Education

ACIE-Critical Language Scholarship Program

Beinecke Scholarship Program

Cambridge Overseas Trust

Gates Cambridge Trust

George Mitchell Scholarships

German Academic Exchange (DAAD) New York

Humanity in Action

IIE - Fulbright, Boren, etc.

Jack Kent Cooke Foundation

James Madison Memorial Fellowship Foundation

Marshall Aid Commemoration Commission

Morris K. Udall Foundation

Paul & Daisy Soros Foundation

The Posse Foundation

Public Policy and International Affairs Program

Rhodes Scholarship Trust

Rotary Foundation of Rotary International

Steven A. Schwarzman Education Foundation

Thomas J. Watson Fellowship Program

Truman Scholarship Foundation

US-UK Fulbright Commission

Winston Churchill Foundation

Woodrow Wilson National Fellowship Foundation

INSTITUTIONAL MEMBERS

Albion College

Allegheny College

Alma College

American University

Amherst College

Appalachian State University

Arizona State University

Auburn University

Augsburg College

Augustana College

Austin Peay State University

Ball State University

Barnard College

Baruch College, CUNY

Bates College

Baylor University

Benedictine College

Bennington College

Binghamton University

Birmingham-Southern College

Boise State University

Boston University

Bowdoin College

Bowling Green State University

Brandeis University

Bridgewater State University

Brigham Young University

Brooklyn College, CUNY

Brown University
Bucknell University
Butler University
California Institute of Technology
California State Polytechnic
   University, Pomona
California State University, East Bay
California State University,
   Los Angeles
California State University,
   Monterey Bay
Canisius College
Carleton College
Carnegie Mellon University
Carthage College
Case Western Reserve University
Central Michigan University
Cerritos College
Chapman University
Christopher Newport University
City College of New York, CUNY
Claremont McKenna College
Clark University
Clemson University
Cleveland State University
Colby College
Colgate University
College of Charleston
College of New Jersey
College of Staten Island
College of the Holy Cross
College of William & Mary
Colorado School of Mines
Colorado State University
Columbia College Missouri
Columbia University
Concordia College

Connecticut College
Cornell College
Cornell University
CUNY Baccalaureate for Unique
   and Interdisciplinary Studies
Dartmouth College
Davidson College
Denison University
DePauw University
Dickinson College
Doane College
Drexel University
Duke University
East Carolina University
Eastern Connecticut State
   University
Eastern Illinois University
Eastern Kentucky University
Eckerd College
Elizabethtown College
Elmhurst College
Elon University
Embry-Riddle Aeronautical
   University
Emmanuel College
Emory University
Fairfield University
Florida International University
Florida Southern College
Florida State University
Fordham University
Fort Hays State University
Franklin & Marshall College
Furman University
George Mason University
George Washington University
Georgetown University

Georgia College
Georgia Institute of Technology
Georgia Southern University
Georgia State University
Gettysburg College
Grand Valley State University
Grinnell College
Gustavus Adolphus College
Hamilton College
Hampden-Sydney College
Harding University
Harvard University
Haverford College
Hendrix College
Hobart & William Smith Colleges
Hofstra University
Howard University
Hunter College, CUNY
Illinois College
Illinois State University
Imperial College London
Indiana University
Indiana University of PA
Iowa State University
James Madison University
John Brown University
John Jay College of Criminal
    Justice, CUNY
Johns Hopkins University
Juniata College
Kalamazoo College
Kansas State University
Kean University
Kenyon College
Knox College
Lafayette College
Lake Forest College

Lebanon Valley College
LeMoyne College
Lehigh University
Lenoir-Rhyne University
Lewis & Clark College
Linfield College
Louisiana State University
Loyola Marymount University
Loyola University Chicago
Loyola University Maryland
Loyola University New Orleans
Lubbock Christian University
Luther College
Lynchburg College
Macalester College
Manchester University
Manhattan College
Marist College
Marshall University
Marymount University
Massachusetts College of
    Liberal Arts
Massachusetts Institute of
    Technology
McDaniel College
McKendree University
Mercer University
Mercyhurst College
Miami University of Ohio
Michigan State University
Michigan Technological University
Middle Tennessee State University
Middlebury College
Minnesota State University,
    Mankato
Mississippi State University
Monmouth College

Montana State University
Monterey Institute of
  International Studies
Montgomery College
Mount Holyoke College
Muhlenberg College
New College of Florida
New Mexico State University
New York University
New York University Abu Dhabi
North Carolina Agricultural and
  Technical State
North Carolina State University
Northeastern University
Northern Arizona University
Northwestern University
Oberlin College
Occidental College
Ohio Northern University
Ohio State University
Ohio University
Ohio Wesleyan University
Oklahoma State University
Olin College of Engineering
Oregon State University
Pace University
Pacific Lutheran University
Park University
Pennsylvania State Behrend
Pennsylvania State University
Pepperdine University
Pitzer College
Pomona College
Portland State University
Princeton University
Providence College
Purdue University

Queens College, CUNY
Quinnipiac University
Ramapo College
Reed College
Rice University
Roanoke College
Robert Morris University
Rochester Institute of
  Technology-AEP
Rollins College
Roosevelt University
Rosemont College
Salisbury University
San Diego State University
San Francisco State University
Santa Clara University
Seattle University
Seton Hall University
Shippensburg University
Skidmore College
Slippery Rock University
Smith College
Southern Illinois University,
  Carbondale
Southwestern University
St. Edward's University
St. John's College, Annapolis
St. John's College, Santa Fe
St. John's University/
  College of St. Benedict
St. Louis University
St. Mary's College of Maryland
St. Olaf College
Stanford University
Stevens Institute of Technology
Stonehill College
Stony Brook University

SUNY at Buffalo
SUNY at Cortland
SUNY at Geneseo
SUNY at New Paltz
Susquehanna University
Swarthmore College
Syracuse University
Temple University
Tennessee Technological University
Texas A&M University
Texas A&M University-Kingsville
Texas Tech
Texas Wesleyan University
Towson University
Trinity College
Truman State University
Tufts University
Tulane University
Union College
United States (U.S.) Coast Guard
  Academy
United States Air Force Academy
United States Military Academy
United States Naval Academy
University College Cork
University College Dublin
University College London
University of Alabama
University of Alabama at
  Birmingham
University of Arizona
University of Arkansas
University of California, Berkeley
University of California, Davis
University of California, Irvine
University of California, Merced
University of California, Riverside

University of California,
  Santa Barbara
University of Central Arkansas
University of Central Florida
University of Chicago
University of Cincinnati
University of Colorado-Boulder
University of Colorado-Denver
University of Connecticut
University of Dallas
University of Dayton
University of Delaware
University of Florida
University of Georgia
University of Houston
University of Idaho
University of Illinois at Chicago
University of Illinois at Springfield
University of Illinois at
  Urbana-Champaign
University of Iowa
University of Kansas
University of Kentucky
University of Louisville
University of Maryland,
  Baltimore County
University of Maryland,
  College Park
University of Massachusetts
  Amherst
University of Memphis
University of Miami
University of Michigan, Ann Arbor
University of Minnesota, Duluth
University of Minnesota, Morris
University of Minnesota,
  Twin Cities

University of Mississippi
University of Missouri-Columbia
University of Missouri-Kansas City
University of Montana
University of Nebraska-Lincoln
University of Nevada, Las Vegas
University of Nevada, Reno
University of New Hampshire
University of New Mexico
University of North Alabama
University of North Carolina at
    Chapel Hill
University of North Carolina at
    Greensboro
University of North Carolina at
    Wilmington
University of North Dakota
University of North Florida
University of North Georgia
University of North Texas
University of Northern Iowa
University of Notre Dame
University of Oklahoma
University of Oregon
University of Pennsylvania
University of Pittsburgh
University of Portland
University of Puget Sound
University of Reading
University of Rhode Island
University of Richmond
University of Rochester
University of Scranton
University of South Alabama
University of South Carolina
University of South Dakota
University of South Florida

University of Southern California
University of Southern Mississippi
University of Tennessee
University of Tennessee at
    Chattanooga
University of Texas at Dallas
University of the Pacific
University of Tulsa
University of Utah
University of Vermont
University of Virginia
University of Washington
University of Wisconsin-
    Eau Claire
University of Wisconsin-Madison
Ursinus College
Utah State University
Utah Valley University
Vanderbilt University
Vassar College
Villanova University
Virginia Commonwealth
    University
Virginia Military Institute
Virginia State University
Virginia Tech University
Wabash College
Wake Forest University
Washington and Jefferson College
Washington and Lee University
Washington College
Washington State University
Washington University in St. Louis
Wellesley College
Wesleyan University
West Texas A&M University
West Virginia University

Western Carolina University
Western Kentucky University
Western Michigan University
Western Washington University
Westminster College
Wheaton College (MA)
Whitman College
Whittier College
Wichita State University

Willamette University
Williams College
Winthrop University
Worcester Polytechnic Institute
Wright State University
Yale School of Management
Yale University
Yale-NUS

Appendix B

Survey of the Profession

In spring 2013, NAFA members were asked to individually complete a Survey of the Profession online. The main purpose of the survey was to collect data to allow NAFA members to approach their institutions with compelling facts in the quest for adequate resources, support, and justification for continued fellowship efforts. We hope the results provide insights into many of the concerns often expressed by NAFA members in regards to staffing, salary, and organization. We received 181 complete responses, and the results are presented below. The data are presented in aggregate form in a way that we believe best represents the intent of the survey, which was to provide descriptive information broken down by major institution categories. The results are merely a descriptive snapshot of our profession and will be used for program-related work; they are not intended to be used for analysis or research purposes or for scholarly publications.

The Survey of the Profession is administered by members of the Professional Development Committee of NAFA: Susan Krauss-Whitbourne, University of Massachusetts Amherst; Dana Kuchem, The Ohio State University, and John Orr, University of Portland.

Gender

Respondents indicated whether they were male or female.

Male	18%
Female	82%

Age

Respondents indicated their current age range.

26–35	21%
36–45	36%
46–55	21%
56–64	17%
65 and over	5%

Race

Respondents indicated whether they were white, Black or African American, Asian or Pacific Islander, Hispanic or Latino, or other.

White	89%
Black or African American	5%
Asian or Pacific Islander	2%
Hispanic/Latino	3%
Other	3%

Education Level

Respondents indicated the highest level of education that they have obtained.

Bachelors or masters degree	52%
Doctorate or terminal professional degree (MD, JD, etc.)	48%

Faculty

Respondents indicated whether they currently hold a faculty position. Results are provided overall and by institution type.

Yes	26%
No	74%

	Public	Private
Yes	22%	31%
No	78%	69%

Tenure with Current Institution

Respondents reported the number of years they have been employed at their current college/university.

0–3 years	27%
4–6 years	16%
7–10 years	17%
11+ years	40%

Tenure in Current Position

Respondents reported the number of years they have been employed in their current position as a fellowship advisor.

0–3 years	52%
4–6 years	19%
7–10 years	13%
11+ years	16%

Fellowship Advising Experience

Respondents reported the total number of years they have worked with fellowship activities.

0–3 years	38%
4–6 years	21%
7–10 years	16%
11+ years	25%

Fellowship Advising Appointment

Respondents indicated what percentage of their employment is attributed to work with fellowship advising.

Full-time	33%
Part-time	67%

Daily Fellowship Workload

Respondents indicated how many hours per day are spent on fellowship activities.

Less than 2 hours	29%
2–7 hours	46%
8 or more hours	23%

Part-Time Salary Distribution

Respondents self-reporting as part-time fellowship advisors indicated what percentage of their salaries is attributed to work with fellowship advising.

Less than 25% of salary	46%
26–50% of salary	38%
51–75% of salary	10%
More than 75% of salary	4%

Title

Respondents indicated their job titles.

Director	48%
Assistant/Associate Director	21%
Coordinator	21%
Other	16%
Assistant/Associate Dean	8%
Dean	3%

Additional Duties

Respondents indicated their job duties other than fellowship advising.

Teaching	37%
Academic advising	36%
Career/preprofessional advising	29%
Honors programming	27%
Undergraduate research	27%
Administering university-based merit awards	25%
Study abroad/international	18%
Scholarly research	12%
Service learning/community outreach	11%

Professional Development

Respondents indicated whether or not they receive funds for professional development, such as conference travel.

Yes	91%
No	9%

Type of Institution

Respondents indicated the nature of their institutions.

Public	55%
Private	45%

Size of College or University

Respondents indicated the number of undergraduate students currently enrolled at their institutions.

Less than 3,000 students	22%
3,000–9,000 students	20%
9,001–20,000 students	17%
20,000 students or more	42%

Student Populations Served

Respondents indicated all populations to which fellowship services are available.

Undergraduates	95%
Alumni	65%
Graduate students	54%
Professional students	28%
Students at regional/satellite campuses	12%

Student Travel

Respondents indicated whether their institutions provide travel funds to students who have been invited for fellowship interviews.

Yes	70%
No	30%

History of Advising

Respondents indicated for how many years dedicated fellowship advising has existed at their institutions.

0–3 years	27%
4–6 years	19%
7–10 years	13%
11–15 years	19%
15+ years	15%

Nature of Office

Respondents indicated whether their institutions have an office dedicated to fellowship advising, or if fellowships are part of the activities of a larger office.

Dedicated office	44%
Part of larger office	56%

Location of Advising

Respondents indicated where fellowship advising is organizationally housed at their institutions.

Office of the Provost/VP for Academic Affairs	32%
Honors program	30%
Other	19%
Office of the Dean/Associate Dean	12%
Career/professional services	7%

Size of Office

Respondents indicated how many employees work on fellowship advising. Part-time employees are indicated as .5. Results are reported by institutional size.

Size of Undergraduate Population

# of Employees	Less than 3,000 students	3,000–9,000 students	9,001–20,000 students	20,000+ students	Overall
Self only	74%	56%	67%	40%	55%
.5–1.5	13%	19%	17%	12%	14%
2–6	10%	14%	10%	29%	19%
6 or more	3%	11%	7%	19%	12%

Budget

Respondents indicated the operating budget (excluding salaries) for their fellowship office or activities. Results are reported by institutional size and again by type.

Size of Undergraduate Population

Budget	Less than 3,000 students	3,000–9,000 students	9,001–20,000 students	20,000+ students	Overall
Less than $1,000	37%	25%	48%	27%	32%
$1,000–3,000	29%	16%	15%	13%	18%
$3,001–6,000	16%	25%	22%	13%	18%
$6,001–15,000	16%	22%	15%	34%	24%
$15,000 and over	3%	13%	0%	13%	9%

Institutional Type

Budget	Public	Private
Less than $1,000	39%	25%
$1,000–3,000	13%	24%
$3,001–6,000	14%	20%
$6,001–15,000	26%	22%
$15,000 and over	9%	8%

Salary

Respondents indicated their annual salary in their current positions. The average salaries are reported below. The data indicates salaries for faculty separate from non-faculty and is broken down by type and size of institution.

Institution Type	Undergraduate Population	Non-Faculty	Faculty
Private	< 3,000 students	$58,640	$71,560
	3,000–9,000 students	$60,280	$82,810
	9,001–20,000 students	$57,500	$125,000
	20,000 students or more	NA	NA
Public	< 3,000 students	$42,500	NA
	3,000–9,000 students	$58,500	$63,130
	9,001–20,000 students	$58,440	$75,630
	20,000 students or more	$62,270	$69,820
Overall		**$58,099**	**$73,882**

Career in Fellowship Advising

Respondents indicated whether they plan to remain in fellowship advising as a career.

Yes	36%
No	16%
Not sure	48%

Career Path

Respondents indicated their intended career paths.

University administration outside fellowships	45%
Fellowship advising	35%
Faculty position	15%
Employment outside academia	5%

Supplemental Questions for Faculty Only

Tenure

Faculty respondents indicated whether or not they have tenure.

Yes	41%
No	59%

Exemption from Committees

Faculty respondents indicated whether they are exempt from most other committee duties because of their various responsibilities with fellowship advising.

Yes	30%
No	70%

Release Time

Faculty respondents indicated whether they receive released time from teaching for their fellowship duties.

No release time	64%
1–25% released	16%
26–50% released	11%
51–100% released	9%

Assessment

Faculty respondents indicated by whom they are assessed for the purpose of their annual reviews.

Administrative unit to which fellowships report	54%
Home academic department	22%
Both administrative unit and academic department	24%

Salary Supplement

Faculty respondents indicated whether they receive a supplement to their base salary for working with fellowship advising.

No supplement	83%
1–20% supplement	11%
21–100% supplement	6%

Supplement Retention

Faculty respondents indicated whether they would retain that base salary if they were not working with fellowship advising.

Yes	71%
No	29%

Salary Retention

Faculty respondents indicated whether they would take a cut in salary if they were not working with fellowship advising.

Yes	11%
No	89%

Index